# The Laughter Factor

The 5 Humor Tactics to Link, Lift, and Lead

## Adam Christing

BK

Berrett–Koehler Publishers, Inc.

Berrett-Koehler Publishers, Inc.
1333 Broadway, Suite P100
Oakland, CA 94612-1921
Tel: (510) 817-2277
Fax: (510) 817-2278
bkconnection.com

## ORDERING INFORMATION

**Quantity sales.** Special discounts are available on quantity purchases by corporations, associations, and others. For details, please go to bkconnection.com to see our bulk discounts or contact bookorders@bkpub.com for more information.

**Individual sales.** Berrett-Koehler publications are available through most bookstores. They can also be ordered directly from Berrett-Koehler: Tel: (800) 929-2929; Fax: (802) 864-7626; bkconnection.com.

**Orders for college textbook / course adoption use.** Please contact Berrett-Koehler:
Tel: (800) 929-2929; Fax: (802) 864-7626.

Distributed to the US trade and internationally by Penguin Random House Publisher Services.

The authorized representative in the EU for product safety and compliance is EU Compliance Partner, Pärnu mnt. 139b-14, 11317 Tallinn, Estonia, www.eucompliancepartner.com, +372 5368 65 02.

Berrett-Koehler and the BK logo are registered trademarks of Berrett-Koehler Publishers, Inc.

Clean Comedians® is a registered trademark. INVERSITY™ Solutions is a registered trademark of Karith Foster.

Printed in the United States of America

Berrett-Koehler books are printed on long-lasting acid-free paper. When it is available, we choose paper that has been manufactured by environmentally responsible processes. These may include using trees grown in sustainable forests, incorporating recycled paper, minimizing chlorine in bleaching, or recycling the energy produced at the paper mill.

**Library of Congress Cataloging-in-Publication Data**

Names: Christing, Adam author
Title: The laughter factor : the 5 humor tactics to link, lift, and lead / Adam Christing.
Description: First edition. | Oakland, CA : Berrett-Koehler Publishers, Inc, [2025] | Includes index.
Identifiers: LCCN 2025003624 (print) | LCCN 2025003625 (ebook) | ISBN 9798890570802 paperback | ISBN 9798890570819 pdf | ISBN 9798890570826 epub
Subjects: LCSH: Leadership—Psychological aspects | Wit and humor in business | Laughter
Classification: LCC HD57.7 .C528 2025  (print) | LCC HD57.7  (ebook) | DDC 658.4/092—dc23/eng/20250604
LC record available at https://lccn.loc.gov/2025003624
LC ebook record available at https://lccn.loc.gov/2025003625

First Edition

33  32  31  30  29  28  27  26  25      10  9  8  7  6  5  4  3  2  1

Book production: Westchester Publishing Services
Cover design: Ashley Ingram
Author photographs: Jack Robert Photo

*For my dad, Paul Duane Brown*

Your laughter inspired me.

Your love anchored me.

Thank you for always showing up.

# CONTENTS

## TACTIC 4   WORDPLAY   84

### USE WITTY LANGUAGE AND CLEVER BANTER.

▼ *It's fourth down, and you're punning.*

## TACTIC 5   AMPLIFY   110

### EXAGGERATE STORIES AND SITUATIONS FOR IMPACT.

▼ *Turn your small tales into tall tales.*

## LEADING WITH LAUGHTER   132

### LET HUMOR OPEN DOORS AND HEARTS IN YOUR ORGANIZATION.

▼ *Because nobody ever said, "I love how serious you are all the time."*

# INTRODUCTION

*What's going on with her?*

The neural circuits in her brain are firing rapidly. She feels an electrifying surge of dopamine. Endorphins are flooding into her bloodstream.

She is taking in extra oxygen.

Her face is contorting. Her body temperature is rising. Suddenly, a burst of sound escapes her mouth at approximately seventy miles per hour.

She feels euphoric.

What's going on here? Has she taken drugs? No . . .

*She's laughing.*

An involuntary reaction that starts just after birth and stays with us until we enjoy our last laugh, laughter is the universal sound of bliss. It ripples through comedy clubs, board meetings, sales gatherings, and Zoom meetings. Funny fuels our social media and sparks viral videos.

We hunger for humor. We pay for it, seek it out, and judge others by how well they can make us laugh. "He has a great sense of humor," or "She brings so much fun to our team."

You get it. Laughter is lit. But . . .

## "What If I'm Not Funny?"

Many think the problem is that others don't think they're funny.

Truth is, the issue is this: *You* don't think you're funny. But you *are*.

You *do* have a sense of humor. But maybe up until now your sense of your own humor style has just gone unrecognized or underdeveloped. Be of good cheer. This book is designed to help you find your funny.

I'll be your host for a joy-filled journey. I know what makes people laugh. I have been in the funny business since I was fourteen. As a professional comedian, funny keynote speaker, and master of ceremonies, I've shared the stage with hilarious comedians like Martin Short and have learned humor tools from some of the funniest people on the planet. I am president of an entertainment bureau called *Clean Comedians*. We represent more than a hundred stand-up comedians, comic-magicians, and dozens of humorous speakers who know how to get big laughs without being offensive.

Laughter may seem random, but in *The Laughter Factor*, you'll discover how to trigger it on demand—whenever, wherever, and with anyone.

I have a message for you. The joke's *in* you. Not only do you have a sense of humor, but a sense of humor has you. Because you are *human*, you are by nature a *humor being*.

This book is your invitation to feel more at home with your own personal brand of humor. You are about to discover five ways of being funny—and one or more of them will fit you. You are about to explore the habits of humorous people—people who make humor *work* for them—and you'll find that you already gravitate toward one of these humor tactics.

Are you someone who likes to surprise other people? Do you enjoy poking fun at others—and at yourself? Or do you get a kick out of delighting friends and associates with inside jokes? Perhaps you like to remember and relive funny moments you've shared with friends. Or you're known for telling larger-than-life stories.

Whichever of these ways of being funny is *you* (and it could be more than one of them), it's time to harness your sense of humor and really dial it in.

Get ready to increase your self-mirth. Do you manage people? Laughter can bring them together. Are you in sales? Funny is money. If you're a leader in your company or field, you know that *leaders bring people together*. And many people are discovering that laughter is a powerful way of creating and forging those links. Do you need to gather your group for an important meeting? Humor helps. Are you a teacher or preacher? According to the American Psychological Association, research shows that laughing leads to learning.

## Make a Splash

Do you remember the first time you stepped onto a diving board? Your heart raced, your legs wobbled, and a million what-ifs filled your head. *What if I belly flop? What if I embarrass myself?* But then, you jumped. Splash! The water embraced you, and your world cheered.

Telling a joke or a funny story for the first time feels like that. It's scary at first—what if it falls flat? But as laughter ripples through the room, you realize it was worth it. And you can't wait to do it again.

When you connect with people with a splash of humor, they will feel linked to you, like being on LinkedIn. And if being funny makes you feel nervous, I got you. In the Q & A section at the back of the book, I give you eight tips for overcoming nervousness.

### Are you a LinkedIn addict like me?

▼ If you've congratulated someone on a work anniversary but don't know where they work . . .

▼ If you posted cat pics during a meeting on productivity . . .

▼ If you've added a hashtag to your middle name . . .

▼ Or if you checked your feed while reading this . . .

. . . you might be a LinkedIn addict.

## We Are Linkers

We see ourselves as thinkers, but at heart, we're *linkers*. And here's some great news:

> Humor is a shortcut to trust.
>
> —*Adam Christing*

(Yes, I just quoted myself. Author privilege.)

And do you know the fastest way to form trust? Through laughter.

Humor isn't just a nice-to-have—it's the missing link for leaders. Laughter skips the formalities and says, "I see you. I get you. I like you."

Here's a story.

I was once invited to sit in on a team meeting. It was going off the rails—negative financial reports, awkward silences, and tension. It felt like there was a dark cloud hovering in that room.

As the guest presenter, I was asked to share "an outsider's perspective."

So I said, "I think we can all agree on the real problem here: Todd's tie!"

(Todd was well known for wearing a different tie to work every day and loved being noticed for it.)

The mood shifted. Stress dropped. Everybody laughed, including Todd.

He laughed the most!

That's the magic of humor. It builds a bridge. It links us together.

Want to connect quickly?

Stop overthinking and start *linking*.

## Your Humor Can Stand Out—Even If You're Not a Stand-Up

In my work as a professional event emcee, I often have the privilege of introducing CEOs, *New York Times* bestselling authors, celebrities, and entertainers. Through these experiences, I've discovered a concept that can truly change the game: the *laughter factor*. Humor is more than just a tool to lighten the mood; it's a transformative force that reshapes how you connect with others. Whether you're breaking the ice in a meeting or building bonds with friends, humor forges stronger connections and enhances experiences.

*The Laughter Factor* may not make you a celebrity, but it will help you shine as a leader, manager, or communicator. I'm going to show you how to harness your sense of humor so that you can

▼ feel way more comfortable making people laugh
▼ learn to lead with humor
▼ boost your sense of well-being as you bust people up

Aside from (possibly) funerals and breakups, I can't think of any situation where tapping into your sense of humor will make things worse—*if you know how to use it*. And I'm going to show you how. You'll read some funny stuff, gain some great tips, and zero in on your special "laugh language."

It's hard to stay mad at someone who's making you laugh or smile! Once, when I was a kid, there was a big bully boy chasing me around on the playground. He wanted to punch me. I hit him with some punch lines I had learned from joke cards I had memorized. Instead of punching me in the stomach, he started busting a gut himself. We are still friends to this day!

Humor helps.

I'll also show you how to be a better giver and receiver of the good times that laughter brings. But the biggest plus of all may be how using the laughter factor equips you to empower others. You will also find that people are more drawn to you when you make them laugh. And with these humor strategies, you'll know exactly how to do it.

The verdict is in from health practitioners, business researchers, and even Nobel prize–winning physicists like Richard Feynman, who said: "We laugh, we joke, we live."

Along with the tips and tricks of humor, I am going to show you many things *not* to say or do when it comes to using your sense of humor. You'll also learn to overcome the fear of *trying* to be funny. Get this: You already are funny—even if you don't believe it . . . yet.

At the end of each chapter, I assign you some humor homework. (Relax. No grades will be given.) There are practical ways you can implement what you learn here, and I'll give you easy-to-use ideas to incorporate the laugh lessons that we discover together. I'm going to stress that word again. *Together.* You and I are embarking on a journey that will take us beyond jokes, gags, puns, and funny storytelling. We are going to understand how laughter brings people together.

I believe you'll start to see yourself in a whole new and wonderful way, as a *humor being.*

Because being funny means being more of who you already are.

That reminds me of a classic joke:

Landon was way out of shape. He was about a hundred pounds overweight, and he was not happy about it. He prayed, and he heard God's voice say, "You can be whoever you want to be."

He decided to get healthy. So, Landon joined a gym. He started riding a bike to work. He stopped eating red meat. He cut sweets out of his diet. He switched from soda to water with lemon.

It worked!

Landon lost all those extra pounds. He slimmed down and even got a cool haircut to celebrate his new look. Then he bought new clothes and got a tan!

One day, as he was walking out of the tanning salon, Landon was hit by a truck and died.

When he got to heaven, he asked God: "What happened? I worked so hard. How could you have done that to me?"

And God said, "Sorry, Landon. I didn't recognize you!"

When you learn to have fun with the five humor tactics I'm about to teach you, things will change for you, too. But unlike Landon, you will be recognized—for how you make people feel.

And people will tell you, "I like the way you make us feel."

I'm glad we are on this journey together. I'm excited this book found you. I also hope you paid for it!

## Before We Get Started

There's nothing quite like the buzz you feel when you tap into your sense of humor. The burst of laughter you generate is bliss for those laughing—and for you.

And, let me emphasize that you don't have to rely on dirty jokes. Everything you're about to read is safe for work and won't get you in trouble at family dinners. "Fun" is not a four-letter word. I'm going to show you how to be funny—without getting fired.

We'll go over proven strategies that are easy to weave into your daily life and career. Even better, at least one of these laugh languages is going to match your personality. (And if not, no worries—awkward silences can be funny too. More on that later. . . .)

## The Five Laugh Languages

Have you read the runaway bestseller *The 5 Love Languages* by Gary Chapman? It's about identifying how to communicate in a way that helps people feel loved. I gave a copy to my youngest son James, and after he read it, I asked him, "What's *your* love language?"

Without even pausing, he said, "Venmo!"

This book is a guide for understanding your sense of humor and learning how to express it. To do that, we are going to identify your favorite laugh language. You will discover your go-to humor tactic—maybe more than one—and learn how you can most effectively use laughter to link, lift, and lead the people around you.

Ready to laugh for a change? These five *fun*damental humor strategies will do the trick:

▼ Surprise!
▼ Poke
▼ In-Jokes
▼ Wordplay
▼ Amplify

You will experience "Ha ha!" and "*Aha!*" moments as you begin to see yourself as a humor being. I start each chapter with a joke that conveys the essence of that particular laugh-generating tactic. At the end of each chapter, I give you some humor homework. There are checklists you can go through to identify your smile style.

"Schtick" is an old term comedians use to describe their special way of making people laugh. I will help you walk tall and carry a "big schtick." When you embrace your way of being funny, you'll be laughing all the way to . . . better relationships and results.

Every good nonfiction book offers you a promise. I'm going to top that.

I am offering you a guarantee: If you read this entire book and don't find it helpful and funny, I'll personally refund your money. And by "personally," I mean you'll have to find me.

So, let's get started. Laughter can be a bridge for connecting hearts. Let's cross it. Together. I will meet you in these pages. Before you turn the last page, you'll uncover the hidden key to all great humor. I'll be your guide—your *sensei* of humor—as I show you how the laughter factor can open doors and hearts in business and in life. *Laughing matters*.

Get ready to turn the humdrum into "Ha ha!" Let's face it. Laughing is way more fun than crying, and it makes you feel good. Like a magic trick, creating laughter is easy, once you know the secrets.

Let's get this party started.

# WHAT IS THE LAUGHTER FACTOR?

## LEARN WHY HUMOR IS THE CURRENCY OF CONNECTION.

A few years ago, I was hired to entertain the guests at a stunning wedding in the Bahamas. The mother and father of the bride had chartered a private jet from Houston to Nassau. When I got off the plane, I saw my friend Jay Mincks. As the senior vice president of a multibillion-dollar company called Insperity, he was managing a sales force of 650 business performance advisors.

Jay saw me at a distance. Before he even said hello, I saw him grab his cell phone and text his company's meeting planner. "Get Adam Christing for our sales convention. He brings the laughter factor." That moment planted the seed for this book.

I named this book *The Laughter Factor* because, after giving more than four thousand different humor-packed presentations and introducing dozens of humorous speakers and variety performers, I know firsthand that laughter is magic. But don't worry. You don't have to be a professional comedian to find your way of being funny. I'll say it again: *Humor* is *human*. This book will help you harness your sense of humor and leverage the laughter factor in your life.

So, what exactly is the laughter factor? It's the ability to

▼ walk into a room and know you can lift the mood
▼ give a presentation and feel confident people will enjoy it
▼ take painful situations and make them feel playful
▼ make a point that sticks because you've made it memorable
▼ cause milk to squirt out of people's noses

In short, it's the ability to use funny as fuel to take you much further in your personal and professional relationships. This book won't turn you into a comedian, but it will give you the strategies that make people smile, laugh, and lighten up.

To experience the laughter factor, you simply need to

▼ commit to using your unique "laugh language"
▼ choose from the humor tactics I will teach you in these pages
▼ find your favorite ways to be funny and start using them immediately

Embracing the laughter factor transforms both you and the situations you encounter. Humor boosts creativity and resilience, strengthens relationships, and becomes your go-to ally in navigating life's challenges. While you can't control everything life throws your way, you can choose to respond with a smile—and that makes all the difference. Humor unlocks possibilities and deepens connections wherever you go.

Let's be real. Humor doesn't change *everything*. But it always changes *something*. And that something is vital. Laughter instantly connects us and opens our hearts and minds!

In this book, we will do more than evaluate humor. My goal is to help you enhance your ability to humor yourself and those around you. What you learn in these pages will help you experience the true meaning of laughter: feeling connected to other people.

This book is for managers, community leaders, trainers, speakers, teachers, preachers, sales peeps, group managers, and anyone who wants to enhance their ability to connect and communicate through humor. You're going to experience *the amazing relational benefits of humor.*

You won't find any political humor in this book. (You're welcome.) Here's why: Politics divides us, but laughter can unite us.

Wait. I will tell you one political (sort of) story. When I was in eighth grade, one day I was gambling with my friends in the boys' restroom. When I got back to class, the teacher called me over. "The vice principal wants to speak with you right away."

I thought I was busted.

I sat in Mr. Fred Luedtke's office, trembling, my pants pockets loaded with about thirty quarters from my gambling earnings. Then Mr. Luedtke looked me straight in the eye and asked, "How would *you* like to run for student body president?"

Fast-forward to my big campaign speech. I cracked jokes. I poked some light fun at one of my beloved teachers, Mr. Grandi, who had a great head of hair, a very cool perm. I said, "Some people have a hairdo. Mr. Grandi has a hair don't."

I made fun of myself. I pledged that I would legalize pencil fights. The kids laughed.

My opponent protested. "Do you really want a clown as your student body president?"

The voters at Granada Middle School said yes.

But this book is not about my wins or losses, though I will share some stories about both. *The Laughter Factor* is about how you can open hearts in business and in life by developing your own sense of humor.

You might be wondering, *How come I've never heard of this Adam Christing guy?* I'll tell you why right up front. I'm not quite famous—but I am funny. I have used all five of the humor tactics I'm going to teach you here to build a career in comedy, stand before over a million people at live events, and reach millions more through TV, radio, podcasts, and funny postcards to my grandkids . . . And I can show you how to be more humorous, too.

Oh, here's just one of the reasons I'm not a big name. I make my humor all about making *other people* look and feel good. Sure, I get a lot of laughs, but I choose to do it in a way that makes other people get the applause as managers, event coordinators, sales trainers, church leaders, and nonprofit executives.

My agent does not like this choice.

## Raise Your RIZZ with Humor

Want to stand out, win people over, and maybe even get Pam from payroll to finally crack a smile? Comedy isn't just for stand-ups—it's your secret charisma booster. Here's an acronym to raise your RIZZ with the laughter factor:

> **Relatable.** Humor helps people see you as human, not just part of a to-do list. In-person meeting? Laughter breaks the ice: "Finally, a meeting where I don't have to mute myself while snacking!"
>
> **Interactive.** Smiles are contagious—but you have to go first. Laughing with (not at) people makes you feel more connected. It's hard not to like someone who makes you laugh. And it's even harder not to love someone who laughs with you.
>
> **Zany.** A dash of unexpected humor boosts positive energy online and offline. Making a presentation? Toss in a surprising one-liner, like "This graph is so colorful, it doubles as my vision board."

**Zest.** Come ready to play. You don't have to be an entertainer to crank up your enthusiasm. It's infectious!

Humor makes you more magnetic. When people link you with laughter, it catapults your charisma.

Ready to raise your RIZZ as a leader? To harness your humor? Here we go . . .

## TACTIC 1

# SURPRISE!

### DELIGHT PEOPLE WITH THE POWER OF THE **UNEXPECTED**.

A somber church service has begun. The minister steps away from the pulpit.

He faces the congregation and starts singing, a cappella, "I am the senior minister of this church. I make three thousand dollars a month . . . that's not enough money."

A minute later the youth minister steps forward and chants his song to the assembled flock:

"I am the youth minister of this church. I make fifteen hundred dollars a month . . . that's not enough money."

Finally, it's the church organist's turn. He sings,

"I am the organist of this church. I make ten thousand dollars a week . . .

THERE'S NO BUSINESS
LIKE SHOW BUSINESS!
LIKE NO BUSINESS I KNOW!"

Almost as much as they love to laugh, *people love to be surprised.* Surprise is a fantastic tactic for bringing the laughter factor to any setting. In this chapter, you'll learn how to put the unexpected to work for you.

The best comedians have surprising "hooks." Often, it's their point of view that surprises people. As a comic, I like to interact with an audience. But I don't perform raunchy comedy. Instead, I like to surprise them with the way I introduce myself.

## Please Allow Me to Introduce Myself

They call me "Mr. Brightside." Actually, that's what I call *myself.*

I used to struggle with depression. Sometimes I still do. Depression is a very real thing for millions of people. For me, after I read *Man's Search for Meaning*, I realized what was going on with me. I had an attitude problem. Viktor Frankl survived a concentration camp. And here I was, complaining about my iPhone 17.

I'm always looking for the upside. Life becomes so much better when you think of yourself as a human highlighter. You have heard of "paranoia." I have developed a condition called *pro*-anoia. I believe the whole world is secretly conspiring to make me happy.

For example, the other day I found a DVD I'd rented that was twelve years past due. I owe them $857. . . . But on the bright side, it was from Blockbuster. Good luck collecting that fee!

Sure, tough things happen to me too, but I try to find the silver lining. Just last week, my brand-new Mercedes-Benz was stolen. On the bright side, it was a rental.

Life is full of ups and downs, and sometimes you just have to roll with the punches. I just spent three hours with the dentist . . . selling him Amway.

And speaking of unexpected twists, there's a crack in my swimming pool. The good news? I *have* a swimming pool! My favorite aunt just married a real jerk, but here's the thing—he fixes pools.

Of course, like everyone else, I face challenges. I just had my identity stolen online . . . and wouldn't you know it, that guy is getting audited by the IRS. Talk about karma! And then there was the time I was in L.A. and got carjacked all the way to San Diego. On the bright side, we got to use the express lane. Even painful incidents have their perks.

Sometimes the little annoyances can really get to you, like that salesman who was driving me nuts, telling me that if I gave him fifteen minutes, he could save me 15 percent on my auto insurance. So I gave him half an hour . . . and saved 30 percent.

Sometimes it's all about finding the humor in the situation. Thanks for laughing, but I know how it is when I'm not around—you'll be saying *nice things* about me behind my back. Speaking of which, our dog ran away. One down, three to go.

Car problems? Yeah, I have those, too. I got a ticket for parking in front of my house on street-cleaning day. Here's the upside: My rims and tires are spotless now. And just the other day, I got two flat tires. It felt fantastic because the guy who was class president and star quarterback at my high school was driving the tow truck. Talk about a blast from the past!

Even when things get really frustrating, like getting into a fender bender with a doctor and not being able to find my insurance papers, I try to see the bright side. It was wonderful—I got to make an MD wait.

And when my next-door neighbor's house fell into a sinkhole, it wasn't all bad. Great news: His dog quit going in our yard!

Life throws curveballs; people aren't always there for you. I know you're talking about me behind my back, and I love the things I imagine you're saying.

I like to think of myself as someone who's always *breaking glad*. When my dentist discovered my gums aren't healthy, he was so impressed he put my plaque on his wall!

When I was on hold with the phone company the other day, the recording said, "Your call is important to us." And you know, just hearing that *I* was that important to a giant multinational company—that just made my day.

Sometimes it feels like I can't lose. Cops often pull me over . . . just to say hello.

But, yes, things can fall apart. My watch stopped working recently. On the bright side, nobody has looked at a watch since 2002. My GPS stopped talking to me, but that's fine—she was kind of bossy, always trying to tell me where to go.

Hey, I know you're saying things about me behind my back. But I'm just glad my name came up!

## Your Secret Weapon

The monologue you just read is my schtick. Your schtick will be based on your point of *you*—your lens on life that makes your material funny. But before we go any further, let's talk about something that's not so funny.

*Chess.*

Wait! Don't stop reading . . .

Did you watch *The Queen's Gambit*? Chess is a serious game, but it's full of surprises—just like an unexpected joke.

Surprise in humor works just like a sudden, unexpected move in chess. It changes the game—and sets you up for a big win. And the other person doesn't feel defeated; you've actually made them feel happy.

Checkmate! Whether it's a punch line that comes out of nowhere or a twist nobody saw coming, *surprise* is your secret weapon for keeping things fresh and funny. And honestly, who wouldn't rather win by making people laugh?

A joke is a logical sentence taken to its illogical conclusion. Laughs come when we make a pattern and then break that pattern. Every list is a setup waiting for a punch line:

1. Pick up the in-laws.
2. Go to the bank.
3. Pick up therapy brochures.

Life is full of these lists. Piles of stuff on top of stuff. But buried in the back of our minds is a little firecracker of astonishment we've forgotten is there. Humor is the fuse that reignites that spark of astonishment. And laughter is the sound it makes when it goes *boom*! It feels good to be alive when you are laughing. And the great thing about this tactic of surprise? You can use it even if you are not a natural joke-teller.

## His Name Is Earl

How did a "humorless" and seemingly boring guy named Earl Nelson make his customers laugh again and again? Earl was dry. His speech pattern was monotone. But for many years, I saw him standing behind the counter at the old Hollywood Magic shop as he demonstrated card tricks for tourists who had wandered in. He had people laughing out loud.

Earl never told jokes, never raised his voice, and never ever acted silly. Yet somehow, this mild-mannered man would always make 'em laugh. Many times, I watched his onlookers howl with laughter.

What secret did this magician understand about the laughter factor? *Surprise!*

Earl Nelson was a master of sleight of hand. Every trick he performed ended on a knockout punch. He would invite you to "Take a card, any card." And somehow, while you were holding that king of hearts right in your hands, *poof*! It would vanish. Aces would explode out of the deck. Earl could make a playing card eerily move toward you—like the deck was haunted. He blew people away. Their jaws dropped. But their first reaction was not applause. They *laughed*.

A good magic trick makes you laugh because it surprises you. In *Variations*, the book Earl Nelson wrote for magicians, he states: "A good effect usually makes people laugh, out of astonishment, even though nothing funny was said."

## Have a Ball

You don't have to be a magician or a stand-up comedian to wow people with the humor tactic of surprise. It's simple, if you have the nerve. Astonish people with what you wear, do, or say. Unexpected twists are at the heart of humor.

My mom has the superpower of surprise as her way of being funny. She would say things like, "Out of the mouths of babes, often comes . . . oatmeal." The great comedians of yesteryear knew how to surprise their listeners. Henny Youngman built his entire career around four words with a twist at the end: "Take my wife . . . please."

Maybe wordplay is not your thing. You can still enjoy the power of wow. My friend Robert Channing is a mind-reader. (I love to kid him. Years ago, I called him from a pay phone. He asked, "Who's calling?" I said, "Hey, *you* tell *me*!") Robert blows people's minds by revealing all kinds of things he couldn't possibly know. He can name your childhood pet or tell you your driver's license number—while he's blindfolded! What I learned from him that most amazed me is the impact of delighting clients with an unexpected gift that makes them grin.

Robert turned me on to something you can buy at Walmart or other big-box stores: *bouncy balls*. We send them to our event planner clients at AdamChristing.com. You can too—via snail mail! That's right. Instead of sending a thank-you note—which is always a great idea, but *predictable*—send them a giant bouncy ball. It's easy to do. Grab a marking pen. Handwrite a note right on the ball: "Heather, we had a *ball* with your team at the annual meeting."

Gifts are always a great idea. And sure, you can send chocolate. That's sweet. We have mailed gift baskets to customers. Greeting cards. *Zzzzzz*. But imagine the reaction people have when they receive a giant $3 bouncy ball—not to mention the smile on the face of the mail carrier delivering it.

## Bringing Joy by Surprise

I tell our team to make our clients SAD. I'm the president of a business meant to bring people laughter, so why would I say this? Because SAD is our team's term for "surprise and delight." If you like to send unexpected gifts to friends, family, and colleagues, surprise may be your humor tactic—even if you are an introvert.

Sending bouncy balls in the mail may not be the way you roll. Let's explore other ways you can make people glad by *catching them off guard*. Do you have the gift of gab? Sometimes the truth is the most surprising—and funny—thing you can say.

Consider the world of high-priced marketing gurus. Dan S. Kennedy is a legend in these circles; he's known for his *No B.S.* guides to business success. (One of Kennedy's books is *Make 'Em Laugh & Take Their Money*.) When I attended his weekend sales and marketing seminar, he shocked us right from the get-go with his startling humor and honesty. Greeting us, he said, "I'm glad you're here. I'm looking for slow learners with a lot of money." This made us laugh—and want to pay him even more money. This style of true words spoken in jest creates instant rapport. *This guy is the real deal. I love his honesty.* As Rick Reynolds said in his hysterically funny solo show: "Only the truth is funny." And the way you deliver what you are already doing or saying can cause people to laugh and listen up.

When Joe Polish launched his million-dollar-a-year coaching program, he attracted a hundred small business owners who would pay $10,000 a year to attend four quarterly meetings. (Do the math. That's a million bucks in annual revenue.) His coaching clients were invited to attend his mastermind gatherings. He used the power of surprise to wow them. How? *Joe changed the way they received his information.* Most coaches, teachers, and seminar leaders will present attendees with their customary workbook. You know the drill. At the registration table when you arrive, they hand you a name badge and a tote bag filled with swag—aka promotional junk.

But Joe threw his attendees a comical curveball. After attendees found their seats, Joe's event team, dressed as elegant servers, presented his marketing manual to each person on a silver platter. *Pop!* By delivering his information like steak and lobster instead of a nuts-and-bolts workbook, he surprised and delighted his clients. Oh, and he made a million dollars. Imagine how much richer he'd be if he had charged $10,001!

## Before You Hit Send

We were trying to get more business for our funny speakers and entertainment bureau, *Clean Comedians.* I thought I had come up with a brilliant marketing hook for our brand of humor. The voice in my head said, *This will be irresistible.* Spoiler alert: It wasn't.

Here's how it all went down.

Las Vegas hosts hundreds of conventions every year, and I figured I'd struck gold with the perfect headline to reel in those conference event planners. Knowing they were bringing their gatherings to the city of slot machines, I cooked up this gem: "Don't Gamble on the Entertainment at Your Convention."

*I'm a genius*, I thought to myself (since, I'll be honest, no one else was saying it). But then my friend, marketing wizard Brian Keith Voiles—who had one of the biggest hearts of anyone I ever met and a brain about three times sharper than mine—chimed in: "That's clever, but why don't you test it against a different headline?"

I rolled my eyes, thinking Brian was mistaken. But hey, what's the worst that could happen? *Let's test it.*

Enter the revealing world of the marketing "split test." Everything in your ad, sales letter, or pitch stays exactly the same—except for the headline at the top. So, to honor Brian's suggestion, we tried it out. The alternative headline? "Give Your Group the Gift of Laughter!"

_____

**Smiling isn't just a nice gesture. It's a surprising leadership advantage!**

_____

Guess what happened?

My "brilliant" idea pulled in a grand total of zero responses. *Zero. Zilch. Nada.* Meanwhile, the second headline option brought in seven leads! Considering we sent this material to only a hundred event planners, that's a 7 percent response rate. In marketing terms, that's not just good—it's phenomenal. If my headline were a comedian, it would've been booed off the stage. Brian's headline? *It crushed.*

Sadly, Brian is no longer with us, but the lesson he taught me that day is one I will always remember. Brian used to be paid $25,000 to sit down and write a four-page sales letter. He lived in a mansion. But what he loved doing most was giving his wealth, knowledge, and possessions to other people.

He was one of the most generous men I've ever met. Brian's favorite thing to do on a Friday night was to secretly surprise elderly couples by prepaying for their meals at fancy restaurants. He was like a kid in a candy shop when he saw them react with surprise and delight. "This is too good to be true," they'd say. But for Brian, it was always for real. People who love to be generous are the happiest people you will ever know.

Back to the experiment . . .

While my idea was somewhat clever, it was all about how I wanted people to feel about *me.* The secret to surprise laughter—and to leading a successful life, I might add—is how you *make people feel about themselves* and what they receive from you.

Now, let's apply this principle to the sensational power of surprising people with gifts, like my friend Brian loved to do.

## Look What I Got!

Surprising people in a way that's all about them isn't just thoughtful—it's like pulling the rug out from under their expectations (in the best way). You'll leave them smiling, laughing, and maybe even wondering if you hacked their algorithm. That's why this tactic is the first one you should try when applying the laughter factor. Catching someone off guard with a thoughtful gift, joke, or note creates a moment they'll remember long after the wrapping paper's gone.

### *Dos* for surprising gifts:

▼ *Will it delight them?* Make it quirky, fun, or instantly smile-worthy—like personalized socks with their pet's face or a miniature zen garden.

▼ *Is it for them (not you)?* A great gift makes *their* day, not yours.

▼ *Right time, right place?* Send it when they can enjoy it, not when they're juggling chaos.

▼ *Is it special?* Even Amazon gifts feel amazing when you purchase the optional gift wrap and personal note.

### *Don'ts* for surprising gifts:

▼ *No self-promotion.* If it's got your logo, it's not a gift—it's a pitch.

▼ *No confusion.* If it needs a twenty-minute explanation or "some assembly required," skip it.

▼ *No clichés.* Avoid gifts that feel mass-produced or ho-hum.

In the end, it's not just about the item—it's about creating joy. So, surprise someone today and watch the smile spread across their face. Which reminds me . . .

## Grin to Win

Smiling isn't just a nice gesture. It's a surprising leadership advantage! Most smiles are triggered by another smile, so the more you share them, the more likely they are to be reciprocated. They're like little boomerangs of bliss—and unlike boomerangs, they never fly back and smack you on the forehead.

Here's how to lead with your smile:

▼ *Start the chain reaction.* A smile is the universal welcome. Walking into a meeting? Smile. Internet slow? Smile. People are wired to smile back. It's practically automatic. Think of smiles as social Velcro—they make you stickier in the best way.

▼ *Flip the mood switch.* Even when no one's around, a smile can transform your emotional state. A quick grin can turn "Ugh" into "Let's go!" And here's a nice surprise. Even when you "fake" a smile, it doesn't stay fake for long. Soon you're fooling everyone, including yourself.

▼ *Use smiles as your signal.* A smile tells your team two important things: "I'm glad you're here" and "We got this!" It calms nerves, boosts morale, and makes you far more approachable. Bonus: It's the cheapest facelift you'll ever get.

Let me ask you this: *When your people hear your name, does a smile come to their face?*

Now's the time to turn that frown upside down.

Sometimes it's as simple as smiling, even when you don't feel like it. You may not believe you have a million-dollar grin, but every smile has a positive effect on both the sender and the receiver.

## Surprises = Guaranteed Laughs

You might be wondering, *Why is this professional humorist telling me so much about gift-giving?* Here's why: If you surprise people with a gift, I guarantee they will laugh—or at least smile brightly.

This book is about creating fun, not about becoming an effective marketer. But there's a fascinating parallel at play here. One of the most insightful lessons about effective messaging comes from the world of neurolinguistic programming (NLP). NLP experts focus on persuasion. My MD calls it "pseudoscientific nonsense," but whatever your take, they've landed on a powerful truth:

The meaning of communication is the response you get.

What we're after here is moving people into the laughter factor experience—and creating lasting memories of how you moved them. The most important humorist in American history in my opinion, Mark Twain, is credited with observing, "The older I get, the more vividly I remember things that never happened."

But when you surprise your friends, coworkers, bosses, employees, kids—just about anyone you care about (it even works with "enemies")—guess what happens?

*They remember. And they smile.*

Here are some examples of how I use surprise to generate laughter when I am "persuading" people (without their realizing it) to laugh.

### Make the Ordinary Extraordinary

When emceeing an event, I'll walk into the audience and say to an attendee: "Hi. Are you enjoying my work as the event host?" When they say, "Yes," I hand them an iPad-sized device and say, "Great. The screen is going to ask you a couple of questions." The person laughs because we've all been continually asked to tip just about everybody who serves us. Then the audience roars when they see a giant version of the tip screen as a PowerPoint slide:

*15% 20% 75%*
*Custom Tip Amount*
*No Tip (I Am Mean)*

## Show, Don't Tell

I'm often booked to deliver a keynote message called "You Can Do Magic!" Here's how I begin the speech: "When you see a great magician, you might expect him to do something like this." Then I take out a handkerchief and produce a dove right before their eyes! The second surprise? I fold it up and put it in my pocket. (Don't hate me—it's not a real dove, just a latex imitation.) The audience laughs, and I say, "What I'm doing up here is an illusion, but the reality is, you can do magic." This dove gag is far more impactful than simply telling people they can do magic. Don't tell them—show them.

## Flip the Script

Instead of having a business leader give me a formal introduction when I come onstage at her event, I have her say, "And now my friend Adam will introduce our special guest speaker." I walk up to the podium and say, "Our keynote speaker is the author of three personal growth and humor books. He has been featured on more than a hundred radio and TV shows. You're going to love him. Please welcome Adam Christing!" Then I smile wide and say, "Hi! I'm Adam Christing."

Here's a fun example of the opposite joke. You bring on your featured speaker by saying, "Our featured speaker tonight needs no introduction." Then you silently walk off stage. (But don't do that if you want to get asked back as the event host!)

Or if the audience knows you, you could try, "Our next speaker is one of my oldest friends . . . Sorry. One of my *only* friends. Please welcome . . . Adam Christing." (This joke works only if you've made the excellent choice to hire me to speak at your event : )

You can do these things in your world, too. Transform the mundane into something amazing. Wow people with actions that speak louder than words; throw in a delightful twist that catches everyone off guard.

## What Are You Doing to Surprise and Delight Your People?

> We just had a surprise birthday party for my mom's sixty-fifth birthday.
> She was completely surprised . . . because she's fifty!
>
> —*Brad Stine, comedian*

Whether the unexpected is something you send, do, or say, cultivating the humor tactic of surprise works best when it's *intentional*. Surprise celebrations are parties with a purpose. We secretly gather together like we are doing something wonderfully sneaky. Everybody gets super quiet. "*Shhhh!*" Then the moment arrives. The guest of honor walks through the door.

"SURPRISE!"

Two things happen.

The person honored feels stunned. "No way! I had no idea!"

And everybody laughs together as the party is off and running.

We are wired to laugh when we have unexpected experiences. *But springing surprises takes planning.*

Before SeaWorld got into a whale of a lot of trouble because of its poor treatment of captive wildlife, it was doing something smart. SeaWorld used the sensation of surprise to wow families at its aquapark. In one particular show, you'd see trained professionals

## HUMOR HERO: Ann Tatarelli Ulrich

Ann Tatarelli Ulrich is a confidence wingwoman based in Minneapolis, Minnesota. She believes "Confidence is your superpower!" Through her podcast Hello BOLD One and her coaching programs, she helps leaders unlock confidence with playful surprises and vibrant energy.

**Ann's tips for tapping into the power of surprise:**

▼ **Flip the script.** Start your next meeting with a quirky question such as, "Who brought balloons?" It grabs attention right away.

▼ **Be boldly present.** Admit when you don't know something—like those VIP names someone just dropped. Authenticity is startling.

▼ **Add unexpected twists.** Carry something fun, like a mini disco ball, to spark creativity and encourage fresh ways of thinking.

▼ **Celebrate wins with flair.** I use my bold red exclamation-point logo on my business cards and pens as a reminder to stand out. Being bold can be surprisingly fun!

swimming safely with dolphins in a giant pool. Then one trainer would ask for a volunteer to come to the edge of the pool. "Who wants to say hello to Dolphin Daryl?"

A mom—let's call her Julie—would stand up. "I do!"

"Where are you from, Julie?"

"I'm from Kansas City."

And then this fully dressed mom would accidentally fall right into the water with a big splash!

The audience was shocked. *What just happened?* But then, to everyone's amazement, Julie would emerge from the water. And she would perform flawless stunts with the mammals, flipping with them in the air, even performing a synchronized dance with the dolphins. The audience was in stitches as Julie transformed from soccer mom into a spectacular swimmer. It was a moment that left everyone laughing and cheering.

When I was a kid and saw this scene with my dad, we started laughing when we realized it was a planned stunt. "Julie" was a professional dolphin trainer pretending to be a spectator. Dad whispered to me, *"This was done on porpoise."*

If you enjoy the humor tactic of surprise, you can learn to use it on purpose.

Here are some fun ways to spring surprises at work:

**Throw a tax-relief party.** Celebrate April 15th by inviting staff to dress up. Picture coworkers as vampires, celebrities, or patients—it's a blast!

**Change your voicemail.** Delete the boring "Hi, it's Melanie. Leave a message." Instead, record this: "Hi, it's me. Spill the tea!"

**Plan an office potluck party.** Skip the same old holiday feast. Host a "breakfast for dinner" potluck. Think pancakes, waffles, bacon, and donuts at 4:30 p.m. on a Friday.

**Make Mondays mysterious.** Swap your usual team meeting for a surprise activity. Try a scavenger hunt or karaoke, or set up a bowling lane in the break area.

**Do a desk decor swap.** Trade desk gadgets with colleagues for an entire day. Cue the laughter and camaraderie that ensues.

Use good judgment, of course. One surprise you don't want to hear is, "HR would like to speak with you now." But do unleash the power of positive humor where you work and live. Eisai, a human health care company headquartered in New Jersey, hosts a "good humor" day each year to help employees relieve stress and bond together over good clean fun.

The humor tactic of surprise sparks an immediate link to laughter. Look for opportunities to inject surprise into what you are already doing. My friend Greg Hahn, a hilarious stand-up comic, once sent me a greeting card for my birthday. The front of the card had flowers like you'd see at a funeral. It read:

For Grandma during This Time of Sorrow

Inside, Greg wrote:

Happy Birthday, Adam!
Best wishes, Greg
P.S. I can't spend all day running around
trying to find the perfect card.

So, I sent him back this card:

Congratulations on your Bar Mitzvah

And inside it I wrote:

Or whatever bar you visited last night.

What are you already doing? Add some *bam*! Surprise them, and they will smile. When I was in high school, I got tired of writing the same old thing again and again in everybody's yearbook. You know what I'm talking about: "Glad I got to know you this year. Have an awesome summer. Let's keep in touch." So, I bought an ink stamp. When people asked me to sign their annual, I quickly stamped it: "Glad I got to know you this year. Have an awesome summer. Let's keep in touch." Same words. But this funny little stamp delighted my classmates. Decades later, at high school reunions, people still come up to me: "Hey, you're the guy who *stamped* my yearbook!"

Use surprise as your tactic to imprint your brand of fun on people's hearts and minds. In today's world of nonstop spin, sometimes the funniest thing you can say is the plain truth. That's just because the truth has gone retro. But remember, retro is cool. Tell your truth, and people will feel *surprised.* Friendly reminder: If you're dropping truth bombs on other people, add humor—or prepare for the fallout.

## Surprise Statements

A single statement springs a surprise. For example, you could end a staff meeting by inviting each participant to share a bit of wisdom.

"What's the best piece of fun advice you've ever received?"

When it's your turn, you might say:

"My grandfather always likes to remind us, 'If you keep your head while others are losing theirs—you'll be taller than anyone else!'"

Reversal statements work great, too.

When I was a kid, if you were in the principal's office, you were in trouble. Now, it means the principal is in trouble.

Even when it's clean, the best comedy is always disruptive. That's one of the reasons we love to laugh. It breaks up the patterns of boredom and stress in our lives. The best surprising humor jolts us into joy.

## A Single Word Can Be Sensational

The way you end a sentence, emphasizing a single word in a joke or story, can make it funny. For example:

▼ They were engaged for twenty-eight years. He wanted to be *sure.*

▼ I went to a restaurant. They asked me if I had a table preference. I said, "Yes. I'd like to be near a *server."*

Here are three examples of how the corporate comedy duo Scotty and Trink get laughs by emphasizing *one word*:

> I would take a bullet for this woman. So if anyone has a bullet . . .
> I'll *trade*.

And:

**SCOTTY:** I saw her up on that stage, and I instantly fell in love, because she did something no girl had ever done before, and no woman has ever done since.
**TRINK:** I *talked* to him.

And of course:

**SCOTTY:** Trink is short for "Katrina."
**TRINK:** And Scott is short for an *adult*.

Singer Tom Waits liked this one:

> "I'd rather have a bottle in front of me than a *frontal lobotomy*."

OK, that's two words, but you get my point. Here's another of my faves:

> "My uncle lives in a gated community. Prison."

The Russian poet Joseph Brodsky once noted, "Everything that displays a pattern is pregnant with boredom." Sometimes the last word of a joke or a story creates the surprise payoff by breaking a pattern or offering a jolt. James Thurber wrote: "Early to rise and early to bed makes a male healthy and wealthy and dead."

And here's one with a nice twist at the end:

**WIFE:** "Honey, there's water in the carburetor."
**HUSBAND:** "How do you know?"
**WIFE:** "Because the car is in the *pool*!"

## Lacuna Ha Tada

Remember the feel-good song "Hakuna Matata" in Disney's *The Lion King*?

Here's another cool word: *lacuna* (pronounced *luh-KOO-nuh*).

What's a *lacuna*? The word means "a blank space or a missing part." In the study of anatomy, it means "a small cavity, pit, or discontinuity." I know, I know. *Zzzzzz*. But this concept is dynamite for your delivery.

*Insert a hole before your humor.*

This is a powerful humor tool you've enjoyed without even knowing it! Here's how you can use it to add humor to your own storytelling. In this context, lacuna refers to a gap or missing part in a story. When you're telling jokes, this gap invites your listener's imagination to run wild, making the punch line more engaging and effective.

When you set up a joke with a lacuna, you build anticipation and excitement. As your audience guesses what might happen next, your punch line can swoop in to surprise them, challenging their assumptions and sparking laughter. This surprise makes your joke memorable and satisfying.

Timing is everything in comedy, and you can sweeten it with a lacuna. The pause before your punch line heightens the tension. For example, try telling the joke "I told my friend she drew her eyebrows too high"—*pause*—"she looked surprised." Using a lacuna this way makes your joke or story funnier and more impactful!

How long should a good lacuna be? One second less than it would take the savviest person in your group to come up with your punch line.

Now, pause. Take this comical quiz.

## ✓ Is **Surprise** Your Go-To Humor Tactic?

Check the boxes that ring true for you:

❑ I like to shock people with things I say.

❑ I enjoy sending unexpected gifts to friends and colleagues.

❑ I love April Fools' Day!

❑ I'm known for blurting out the funny truth in a situation.

❑ I love movies with twist endings.

❑ I enjoy springing surprises on friends and family.

❑ I see the funny side of things when unexpected events occur.

❑ I like to show up at places unannounced.

❑ Planning a surprise party sounds fun to me.

❑ I'm shocked that I'm still reading this book!

If you checked at least seven of these ten boxes, surprise may be your "laugh language."

This first tactic is at the heart of all good humor. It will make your words and actions *pop*. Tap into this tactic to launch laughter and spark smiles in your personal and professional relationships. When you unleash the unexpected, you will surprise and delight your team.

"Surprise!" The stage is yours.

## Humor Homework

**Link:** How can you use the magic of SAD (surprise and delight) to build a bond with a coworker or new customer? How might you spark a "Ta-da!" moment to turn a casual contact into a connected friend?

**Lift:** Who on your team could use a "Wow!" today? Is there a gift you can deliver to make them laugh and feel as if they just won a Grammy?

**Lead:** What humdrum routine can you shake up to jolt your people into joy? What will you say, do, or wear to create an unexpected dose of fun?

# TACTIC 2

# POKE

## MAKE **FUN** OF YOURSELF AND GENTLY TEASE OTHERS.

The other day at the lake, something incredible happened. I stumbled across a golden lamp. Naturally, I gave it a rub and—poof!—a genie popped out.

He looked at me and said, "I'll grant you one wish. Anything you want."

I decided to go big. "I wish for world peace!" The genie stroked his beard and said, "World peace? That's . . . impossible. Maybe you could wish for something a little more manageable?"

So I thought about it for a minute. "OK then. I wish to *understand myself*—why I forget passwords the moment I create them, why I eat snacks even when I'm not hungry, and why I procrastinate all the time."

The genie said, "World peace it is."

Poking is a powerful humor technique. In this chapter, you'll discover how to make fun of yourself and kid people in a way that makes them laugh—and like you more. And no worries—I'll show you how to deliver jabs and jokes that get people laughing instead of running for cover. We'll explore how to poke fun without risking your friendships, your job, or your sanity.

Here's something you must know, right off the bat: *Humor always has a target.*

Nearly every joke lands *on* somebody, but the best laughs nearly always come from taking aim at yourself.

Nothing says "Can you relate?" quite like reminding everyone of your brilliant idea to try a do-it-yourself haircut before the Christmas party—and the two weeks of hat-wearing that followed.

Self-effacing humor makes us more human, more approachable. You can either laugh at yourself or cry—and laugh lines are far more attractive.

But before we talk about making fun of ourselves, let's take a moment to discuss a favorite subject: making fun of other people!

## Everybody's a Critic

Here's another secret: *Humor is criticism cloaked in fun.*

Dorothy Parker was one of the towering wits of the 20th century. She was known for writing critical jabs that were sharp and funny. As she once put it, "The first thing I do in the morning is brush my teeth and sharpen my tongue." Her reaction to the announcement that President Calvin Coolidge had died was classic: "How can they tell?"

And when reviewing a boring book, she quipped, "This is not a novel to be tossed aside lightly. It should be thrown with great force."

Parker put the *punch* in punch lines. She shows us the key to poke power. Choose your target—then knock it down with a quick jab.

But as a leader, it's even better to criticize yourself in an endearing way. I'll go first.

# Bombing

Here are four times I "bombed" onstage and what I learned about poking a hole in your own ship.

### The Cruise That Sank My Trick

I was hired to entertain guests on a three-hour cruise out of Newport Beach, California. I approached a woman to show her a magic trick.

"Hello. Please pick a card!"

"No thanks. I'm enjoying the harbor view."

**Lesson:** Not everyone wants what you're offering. That's OK—focus on the people who do.

### Class Reunion Chaos

Performing comedy for a twenty-year class reunion sounded fun— until I realized the people there were way more interested in catching up with each other. Nobody was listening to me. "Omigosh, Teri, you look amazing! How are you?"

**Lesson:** The timing might not be right. Don't take it personally.

### Speech Tournament Trouble

I made it to the semifinal round of a National Impromptu Speaking competition. I "killed" with my speech . . . until I pulled out a funny prop. Boom—disqualified. Turns out visual aids were against the rules.

**Lesson:** Know the rules before you get to the gig.

### After-Dinner Show Fiasco

One time when I was performing comedy-magic with an assistant, we noticed that the everyone in the audience was speaking exclusively in Chinese during dinner. I asked her what we were going to do when it was time for us to go onstage. She said, "We're going to bomb. And then we are not going to get paid."

**Lesson:** Learn Mandarin.

## Poke Positive

When KPMG, one of the world's top accounting firms, brought me in for a special assignment, I knew I had a big challenge ahead. My mission? To roast eleven of their top executives who were retiring. Keep in mind, the job of the jester is to rib the king—without getting his head cut off. Yikes!

They hired me to do a one-hour roast (and toast) about all eleven retirees. The challenge? I didn't know any of these people! And I had just two weeks to come up with original material.

*The best humor is sharp enough to pop a balloon but never to break a heart.*

Here's how I pulled it off. First, I interviewed their coworkers. I didn't just ask for generic anecdotes. I dug deep to find the quirks, habits, and unique traits that defined each of these VIPs.

Next, and most important, I identified *one* signature trait for each retiree—something they were known for saying or doing.

Finally, I used the humor tactics in this book to lightly tease them.

The key was personalization. I needed the jokes to resonate not just with the audience but especially with the people being roasted. After all, the goal wasn't just to make people laugh—it was to make these "stars" feel seen, celebrated, and yes, a little roasted. And we all know that being roasted is a recognition that a person *is somebody*. If they weren't, the audience wouldn't have the shared knowledge of their fame *and* foibles. As the roastee sits there, laughing along like the good sport that they are, the audience is encouraged to join in.

I ended up with a full page of jokes for each executive. Since there wasn't enough time to memorize everything, I transferred the material to notecards with the key lines and talking points for each retiree. This way, I could stay on track while keeping the delivery playful and engaging.

Now, I can't share the real names or jokes I used that night—because, well, lawsuits aren't fun—but this will give you a flavor of what went down:

▼ "I'm not saying Jerry drives fast . . . but he bought an E-Z Pass for his speeding tickets."

▼ "Samantha loves wine! She never overdoes it, but I did hear her say, 'You can't buy happiness, but you can buy a case of Yellow Tail cabernet at Costco!'"

▼ "If you want Reggie's attention, you've got to send him a meeting invite labeled 'Urgent Message from Augusta: Golf Outing.' He is avoiding a stroke, not because it will make him healthier, but because he doesn't want to lose to Richard. I hear his favorite number is 'Fore!'"

▼ "Jessica graduated magna cum laude from Yale. She doesn't brag about it. She's subtle: 'Oh, sorry, I didn't mean to Yale at you.'"

▼ "Brice is not a big tipper. I've been told he's single-handedly keeping the 'exact change' industry alive. Rumor has it that he and Melinda added an extra room at their house for his piggy-bank collection."

▼ Tanner was a sharp dresser. I called him onstage and did a funny magic bit where I cut his necktie to pieces. The audience roared. Tanner panicked. Fortunately, I was able to restore the tie. Hey, I wanted to get paid.

These jokes would have tanked at a comedy club! But at the company event, this set "crushed" because I was having good-natured fun with people this audience loved. What was even more important, way more important, was that the retirees felt roasted and revered—celebrated for who they are, quirks and all.

In the end, it wasn't just about the laughs; it was about the love and respect that came through every joke. Poking isn't just about making fun—it's about creating laughs that resonate with those around you.

One more thing: I personally met with each retiree *before* I hit the stage. Why? Because I wanted to run a few of the jokes by them to make sure they liked my angle. This wasn't just about being funny—it was about ensuring that they felt *poked positively*.

Remember, the best roast jokes are the ones that make the "target" laugh even more than the rest of the audience does.

## Be Laugh-Affirming

It's hard to laugh at someone you don't like. Humor works best when it comes from a place of affection, not at someone's expense. When you truly like people, your jokes land softer, funnier, and without the sting that turns humor into hurt.

It's my Golden Rule of positive humor: Don't laugh *at* others. Laugh *with* them.

The point is to poke fun, not to put people down. It's almost never smart to be a smart aleck. When the affection is mutual, the laughter flows effortlessly. Build people up with your humor, and you'll see that the biggest laughs come from genuine connection.

Here are some examples of how to poke fun at others while lifting them:

▼ Julie is so generous—I asked her for the time, and she gave me her watch.

▼ Nina is so thoughtful. She remembered my coffee order . . . from 2022.

▼ Jake is so tech-savvy. He just fixed my mom's Wi-Fi—and she lives in Nebraska.

# ⟶ HAuthenticity

Sometimes I feel like a total phony. My profile pic has been face-tuned so much . . . at the airport TSA asked me for a DNA test.

Then I remember: Our flaws are what makes me—and you—"flawsome."

As a "pro" humorist, comedian, and emcee, you'd think I already knew this. But I've learned something surprising:

The best humor isn't about delivering a polished punch line.

It's about showing up as your real, imperfect self—and embracing your funny failures.

I call it HAuthenticity.

Here's what I've discovered:

▼ Humor happens when you stop pretending to have it all together.

▼ HA has a funny way of showing up just when you need it most—*if* you let it.

▼ And the best laughs? They're enjoyed *with* people, not aimed *at* them.

I want to live with more HAuthenticity—not just onstage but in life.

Make your jokes *laugh-affirming*. Build people up instead of putting them down. Sure, you can stick out your tongue, but make sure it isn't too sharp!

## Lightly Roasting Others

The French philosopher Voltaire wrote, "Lord, make my enemies ridiculous." But in our day-to-day humor, we're not usually dealing with enemies—we're just trying to get a laugh.

The key is to roast lightly, not to burn. This isn't about biting sarcasm that leaves scars. Aim for the kind of fun that makes everyone, including the target, chuckle. A little friendly jab can break the ice and keep the mood light, as long as you know where to draw the line.

Here's a communication rule worth remembering:

*Say what you mean, but don't say it mean.*

Humor is a double-edged sword. If it's too harsh, it cuts deep and can cause real pain. When used playfully, poking can be a tool for bonding. The best humor is sharp enough to pop a balloon but never to break a heart.

This reminds me of a joke:

A man bought a new pet parrot. Excited, he asked the bird, "Can you talk?" The parrot looked him up and down and drawled, "Oh great, another podcast host."

Now, that's sarcasm done right—sharp enough to be funny but light enough to keep everyone laughing. We're dealing with people, not parrots. The lesson: A well-placed poke can spark a nice laugh, and it can all be in good fun.

When it comes to targets, the best one is looking at you in the mirror . . .

## Let Me Ask You This

Whether you are lightly roasting those around you or making fun of yourself, here's a tool you can use: you can poke with provocative questions.

Do you realize how powerful questions are?

Humor is a hook, and questions reel people right in. Master humorists and storytellers *ask lots of questions.*

Your questions can be funny—and they can help you make a point. Influencers like Anthony Robbins, business wiz Gary Vaynerchuk, and historic figures like Eleanor Roosevelt, Martin Luther King Jr., Winston Churchill, even Socrates—*especially Socrates!*—used questions to grab attention.

And get this: Jesus of Nazareth asked 307 questions. He answered only three! By the way, some of the questions he asked were humorous in his day. "Why do you try to take a speck of dust out of your friend's eye when you have a *log* jutting out of your own?"

Are you tapping into the power of questions to spark laughter and learning?

## Employment Annoyment

Be gentle in your jabbing. Here's the fine line: You can make fun of the work but not the workers. As I write these words, I am headed to Montana to deliver a humor keynote to an association of electricians. (Exciting, I know. Especially if circuit breakers and single-pole switches light you up.)

Here's what I plan to have fun with and what I plan to avoid. There are some takeaways for you, no matter what kind of work you do.

I will talk about the long distances these specialists have to drive and the vast assortment of podcasts and audiobooks that help them pass the time. We'll poke some fun at the silly questions they get asked, such as, "Is it OK for my child to lick our outlets?" and "Is it safe to listen to my portable radio in the tub?" And, of course, I'll josh them about how they get to work outside all the time—in the heat, rain, and snow. "Lucky you," I may say, "trading in the comfort of an air-conditioned office for the thrill of standing on a metal ladder during a lightning storm."

But here's what I won't get into: I will avoid making fun of the value they create, their work ethic, or their pay. When it comes to sensitive topics, forget about it. Unless you're an insider (see tactic 3, in-jokes), it's best to keep your comments in the safe zone. No one wants to be the person who turned a special event into a big bummer.

Yes, work can be frustrating—we've all been there. Whether it's the endless meetings that could've been emails or the "urgent" tasks that somehow always land on your desk at 4:59 p.m. on a Friday, work has its ways of testing your patience. Sometimes, the best way to cope with the daily grind is to poke some fun at it.

Here are some wonderful examples of people poking and joking about their bosses and jobs:

> My boss at Christmas was a lot of fun. "I want you to look in your pay envelopes, and you'll know that I keep the spirit of Christmas around here. Because in each and every envelope you'll find . . . snow."
>
> —*Dave Ketchum*

> WARNING TO EMPLOYEES: Firings will continue until morale improves.

> I used to sell life insurance. But life insurance is really strange. It's a weird concept. You really don't get anything for it. It works like this: You pay me money. And when you die, I'll pay you money.
>
> —*Bill Kirchenbauer*

Here's a not-wonderful example: Allison, a newbie district sales manager, was asked to speak at her company's big customer event. Scanning the crowd, she said, "I don't see Arlington Suppliers here. Great—I can finally stop using small words!" A few people laughed. Her VP of sales didn't. Arlington was a former client they were trying to win back. And one of their reps was in the room. Yikes. Remember my rule: *If in doubt, leave it out.* Allison kept her job—but wanted to change her name tag that day. Choose clean fun over mean fun. And always know who's in the room.

Work humor thrives on the shared experience of "employment annoyment." Whether it's the boss who thinks 24/7 availability is part of the job description or the office printer that jams right when the report is due, there's plenty to poke fun at.

So the next time work gets on your nerves, come up with a little poke joke. Then share it with your colleagues—it just might help everybody get through the day.

## The Joke's on You

Long before Amy Schumer was cracking people up, Phyllis Diller was one of the first mega-popular female stand-up comedians, and like Dorothy Parker, she was a master of the sharp jab. Describing her overweight mother-in-law, she quipped, "She's like Jell-O with a belt."

But beyond her sharp punches, Diller was known for something even more endearing: self-mockery. Roseanne Barr aptly described her as "a victorious loser," a woman who turned her own flaws into comedic gold.

Diller's self-deprecating humor is legendary. Here are some "killer Dillers":

▼ "My photographs don't do me justice—they look just like me."
▼ "You know you're old if your walker has an airbag."
▼ "My cooking is so bad, my kids thought Thanksgiving was to commemorate Pearl Harbor."

These jokes aren't just funny—they're relatable. Diller's ability to poke fun at herself made her not just a comedian, but someone audiences could connect with on a deeper level.

You may never land a comedy special, but you can still achieve something just as powerful. By bringing yourself down a few notches, you give others the chance to build you back up in their estimation, and you invite them to relax by learning to laugh at themselves.

And at the end of the day, if they're laughing, you're winning.

## Connect before You Crack

In the world of stand-up, timing is everything—and that's not just about delivering punch lines. Before my comedian friends dive into their sets, they often spend a moment or two connecting with the crowd. It's like establishing a rapport before they start poking fun—they're building a connection by lightly roasting the locals.

Picture this: You're at a comedy club in Philadelphia, and the comic steps up to the mic.

"What's with all the construction here in Philly? I felt like a rat in a maze. I was starting to hope there'd be cheese at the end of it."

The crowd cracks up because they know exactly what he's talking about—the city's never-ending construction work. Then he adds, "And don't even get me started on all the politics here. I'm not saying it's confusing, but I think I just accidentally voted for my Uber driver."

By this point, the audience isn't just laughing; they're nodding along, thinking, *This guy gets us.* They feel understood, like the comedian is one of them. *He knows where I live!*

This approach works because positive humor isn't just about making people laugh; it's also about making them feel connected. When you tap into those shared experiences, people feel more than entertained—they feel drawn closer together.

It's the difference between teasing someone from a distance and gently ribbing a friend who knows it's all in good fun. The latter is where the real connection happens.

So the next time you're about to poke fun at someone, remember to bond with them first. You'll lighten the mood and strengthen the relationship.

Good road comics ask questions of the locals before they go onstage. "What's the restaurant everyone goes to late at night around here? Which nearby small town do you all make fun of? Which smaller town do *they* make fun of? What teams do you all root for? What teams do you all hate? What's new here in town? What's really, really old?"

> ## HUMOR HERO: Mary Anne Kristan
>
> As IT product manager at Public Consulting Group in Chattanooga, Tennessee, Mary Anne Kristan knows the power of leading with laughter. "Humor helps us connect. When you notice people's quirks and show you value them, they feel appreciated," she says. "Playful teasing is actually a team-builder—it strengthens bonds and creates a sense of belonging."
>
> **Mary Anne's tips for positive poking:**
>
> ▼ **Start with *yourself*.** "I like to begin by joking about my six names (my full name is Mary Anne Joy Kent Gibson Kristan)."
>
> ▼ **Create nifty nicknames for coworkers.** Just make sure your teammates like them before you share!
>
> ▼ **Set some "house rules" for humor.** Mary Anne says, "In my family, teasing was our love language. Kindness and kidding can make your team feel like family, too."

Comedians ask these questions because they're looking for the appropriate local targets for their jokes (and because they want to know where they can eat after the show).

Performing for a fabulous group of welders in Arthur, Illinois—halfway between Chicago and Kansas City—I asked, "Who here is a Bears fan?" About half the crowd clapped politely. "And who here prefers to *win* football games?" The other half howled.

### Humoring Hecklers

When I was twelve years old, there was a store called "Vicki's Toy Town." Instead of buying Legos or Hot Wheels, I spent my allowance on insults! I started collecting comeback lines from Groucho Marx, Winston Churchill, and Moms Mabley.

While other kids were playing with action figures, I was busy arming myself with witty retorts, ready to counter any verbal jab thrown my way.

When I became a full-time interactive comedian, I sometimes "planted" hecklers in my audience! Believe it or not, most comedians love hecklers. I'll tell you why: People who challenge you in a rude way are "asking for it."

Now, they aren't asking to be offended, shut down, or bullied. But when someone heckles you—granted, this can be super tricky—sometimes it's best to hit back . . . with humor.

Before I show you how to humor a heckler, let's talk about how *not* to handle it. When heckled, "newbie" stand-up comedians often go ballistic. Say, someone in the third row calls out, "Hey, that happened to me!" and they go off on a tirade. That's not being heckled. That's "audience participation."

Being heckled happens when the floor is yours and someone tries to mop you up. As the leader in this situation, you can't let them do that. But don't make these mistakes, either:

▼ Don't go after anyone's race, religion, gender, or physical appearance.
▼ Don't use profanity.
▼ Don't turn someone's little "barb" into a boxing match.
▼ Don't counterattack until your audience is more annoyed at you than the heckler.

So, what should you do?

1. *Acknowledge that you have been interrupted.* "Looks like I'm not working alone up here."
2. *Answer in a way that quickly allows you to regain control.* My friend Steve Bridges had a heckler disrupt his speech at a high school assembly. "You're bald!" said the heckler. Instead of responding with an insult, Steve said, "That's true. As a kid, my

bedroom was downstairs. My mom used to vacuum so much, I started going bald in elementary school!"

3. *Redirect the focus back to your material with a clever comeback.* For example, let's say someone interrupts you during a speech by saying, "You don't know what you're talking about!" You might respond, "Well, that's just your opinion . . . but my kids tend to agree." By acknowledging the heckler and turning the joke on yourself, you disarm them and maintain control of the situation.

4. *Sometimes you need to repeat what the heckler said before responding.* Remember, the heckler is facing you, without a mic, so people behind him may not have heard what he said.

Here are some examples of quick comebacks. Notice that the heckler started it, but the funny person ends it—without attacking the heckler.

**STUDENT:** Not fair. You need to give us an extension!
**TEACHER:** Let me just check my "extension" jar . . . oh wait, it's empty.

**AUDIENCE MEMBER:** You are terrible! You can't read my mind.
**MENTALIST:** If I do, will you give me half price?

**PARENT:** That was a foul. Hey, ref, you're rigging the game!
**SCHOOL REFEREE:** If I were rigging the game, I'd make it more exciting.

Use these kinds of retorts as a last resort. The goal is never to offend, but if you are speaking and someone tries to derail you, use a clever comeback to get your train back on the track.

Remember, humor should lift the room, not tear someone down. So the next time someone heckles you, don't panic. Take a deep breath and deliver a response that leaves people laughing—and you back in control.

## Humor Me

Humor thrives on defeat—that is, the *acceptance* of defeat. Some of the funniest things you will ever hear are in places like recovery groups. People overcoming addictions and other hard times learn to laugh at themselves and share their humorous perspective with others.

*Authenticity* is more than a trend on social media—it's here to stay. The people gaining the largest followings aren't just sharing their victories; they're opening up about their pain and defeats.

Sure, it's tempting to post "winning and grinning" selfies taken at fancy restaurants—and that's fine. But if you really want to connect and build a following, both online and in person, *learn to poke fun at yourself.*

Make light of your struggles and how hard you are trying to get over them. Making fun of yourself makes you more approachable, vulnerable, and relatable.

And it doesn't take a lot of effort to find the funny from your own life. Here are a few examples:

- ▼ I tried to reduce stress by meditating daily. Now I'm stressed about how much I'm behind on my meditation!
- ▼ A few years back, I made a decision to reorganize my business. They call it Chapter 11.
- ▼ I lost thirty pounds last year. (*Wait for applause. Then pat yourself on the belly.*) This morning, I found it. (*Tag, squeeze your love handles.*) Along with the other ten I misplaced in high school.
- ▼ I decided to eat healthier. So now my fridge is filled with kale. I never eat it. I mean, if God wanted us to eat kale, he would

have had it come out of the ground deep fried and sprinkled with sugar.

## Make Your Frustrations Funny

Turn your hassles into humor. Transform annoyances into endearing "mad moments." You will score empathy points and laughs.

Here's how to spin life's frustrations into comedic gold.

Start by making fun at your own mishaps. If your morning was a mess, share about it with a mini monologue: "This morning, it was dark in the bathroom, and I accidentally used my toothpaste as hair gel. It was gross, but at least my hair smells minty fresh."

What else is bugging you? Use your frustrations as humor material, like this:

- ▼ I've been thinking *My boss is an idiot!* Then I remembered: I'm self-employed.
- ▼ I'm on a new diet, and now I'm angry at everyone who isn't bacon.
- ▼ I remember this one time I had to stand up in front of my entire second-grade class and apologize for stealing money out of the lunch jar. I don't know who was more ashamed—me . . . or my students.
- ▼ From comedian Steven Wright (renowned for his deadpan, hilarious one-liner style): "When I get really bored, I like to drive downtown and get a great parking spot, then sit in my car and count how many people ask me if I'm leaving."

You'll notice that I included someone else's joke in that list. If you're not a professional comedian, it's OK to use other people's jokes, as long as you credit them. Or if you get a joke from ChatGPT, just say, "A close friend of mine named AI likes to say . . ."

Don't shy away from family frustrations, either: "My two sons decided to make us breakfast this morning. I'm looking at two hours of cleanup when I get home . . . after I help them do their homework and read them a goodnight story from Stephen King."

By focusing on your personal annoyances, you'll craft engaging and relatable jokes and stories. Everyone has their own maddening moments, and turning these into "rant riffs" can help you build rapport with others and keep them laughing.

When life pokes you—poke back!

## Breaking Glad

Humor is like a natural drug with positive side effects. Maybe we should call it "cope-ium." It doesn't cure what ails you, but it makes your pain entertaining—and more bearable.

You feel bad that you can't find your shoes, until you meet the man with no feet. When your autocorrect doesn't work right, it's still entertaining to your friends on the text chain. Humor changes our perspective immediately. With the laughter factor, *shifts happen*. Silver linings come into view.

President Lincoln loved humor. It got him through the Civil War. He said, "If you're in a hole, stop digging."

I'm telling you to dig *deeper*. If you're in a rut, build a tunnel.

## Laugh at Your Own Expense

This strategy is not new. But it works.

In Saint Augustine's renowned memoir, *Confessions*, he recommended humility: "Do you wish to rise? Begin by descending."

It's never a good idea to roast other people about attributes they were born with or cannot readily change: their gender, weight, ethnicity, or appearance. But you *can* poke fun at yourself in many ways:

▼ People say I'm old. Maybe they have a point. When I was a kid, Iraq was called Mesopotamia, and the Dead Sea was just sick.

▼ I am on a new diet. When I open my fridge, I find myself hesitating . . . like a dog standing in the midst of four trees.

▼ I can't carry a tune. I once sang in the church choir. Two hundred people left our church.

▼ Yes, I am short. I stopped wearing cowboy boots. They gave me a rash—under my armpits.

▼ I'm a fearful person by nature. When I book an airline ticket, I look for a plane that has two restrooms and a chapel.

▼ I'm not the most thoughtful person. My husband said I ruined his birthday. How is that possible? I don't even remember when it is.

It's not just slinging rapid-fire zingers (more about those in tactic 4, wordplay). You can introduce yourself to a group in a self-effacing way. People love it—and they will instantly feel a bond with you.

Poking at yourself might feel risky. But you will find that your listeners love it. Say the word "intimacy" to yourself slowly. It sounds like this: "*into-me-see.*" When you raise your vulnerability, you will increase your ability to link with others and make them laugh.

To get to the next level in your ability to make people laugh (in your life and career), you simply have to open up your heart more to other people. Humor helps you do just that.

## Take Yourself Down a Peg

I like the term "self-effacing humor." Some call it self-deprecating, but that sounds like a digestive problem. Whatever you choose to call it, you can take yourself down a peg on purpose.

The most winsome humor happens when you poke fun at your own failures and foibles. You *can* laugh at yourself. If you think you can't, call me—I'll do it.

Go ahead. Take some hot air out of your own tires. Joke about your parenting:

▼ I was doing Ancestry.com with my husband. We traced our ancestors back three hundred years but had no idea where our kids were that night.
▼ We've decided to homeschool our kids every day for ten minutes. Starting with recess.
▼ If I had a nickel for every time my kids learned a lesson—not from something I *said*, but from something I *did*—I'd have a nickel.

Here are some (true) examples from my life:

▼ I didn't go to "Promise Keepers" . . . I said I would.
▼ Years ago, I was interviewed by *Success* magazine. I didn't tell the reporter that my car had been towed away the day before because I couldn't make the payments.
▼ As the president of CleanComedians.com, I came up with our company motto: "It doesn't have to be filthy to be funny!" But I blew it. I printed a hundred brochures that went out to businesses, colleges, and associations. There was a typo that I hadn't caught. It read, "*Clean Comedians* is an organization of professional comedians who believe it doesn't have to be funny!" Whoops.

Want to use humor to grow in your relationships at home and at work? People love you more when you let them laugh about the times you felt like a loser.

*Behind every master, there's a disaster.*

It seems counterintuitive, but it's for real. When you make fun of yourself, you actually enhance the way others see, hear, and experience you. Self-effacement is a weird-sounding term. But it's a vital concept. It's the art of showing your humanity through humility.

Poke fun at your own smarts:

"I hate it when people try to act all intelligent and talk about Mozart when they have never even seen one of his paintings."

"For the past twenty-five years, I've received a Valentine's card from a secret admirer. I was upset I didn't get one this year. First my grandma dies, now this!"

Remember, if you laugh at yourself first, you'll beat everyone to the punch.

*Down is up!*

Put yourself down, and the people around you will lift you up. As I like to say, "The first shall be . . . laughed at."

You will find that self-effacing humor is powerful. But it's essential to distinguish it from self-*defeating* humor. The former is about showing humility and connecting with others; the latter can undermine your self-worth and the respect of those around you.

What's the difference? Self-effacing humor says, "I'm human, just like you." Self-defeating humor says, "I'm less than you."

And again, it's not just about poking fun at yourself. Once people know you care about them, you can lightly roast them, too, and they'll feel like they're part of the fun.

It's like holding a marshmallow just close enough to the fire to toast it—warm and a little gooey inside but not burned black outside. This is why roasting, when done right, strengthens bonds rather than singes them.

No one enjoys being the butt of a cruel joke. There's an ancient Latin proverb that remains relevant today: "What is viler than to be laughed at?" But I've learned that laughing at *yourself* can dissolve tension and make you instantly more likable.

Why? Because when you can poke fun at yourself, you show others that you don't take yourself too seriously, and that's a quality people admire—plus, it gives them permission to loosen up around you. And we all need to loosen up a bit. (Unless you're wearing skinny jeans, in which case, good luck.)

## I Like You

Laughing at yourself, and *with* others, makes you instantly likable.

*"My boss says he is going to fire the employee with the worst posture. I have a hunch . . . it's going to be me."*

When you are willing to laugh at your own quirks and mistakes, it signals confidence and security. It's a way of saying, "I'm comfortable in my own skin, and I'm not afraid to show you."

This brand of "poking fun" humor fosters a sense of connection and camaraderie, making people more likely to trust and like you. After all, nothing says "we're in this together" like a shared laugh over how you managed to lock yourself out of your own house . . . again.

## The Sweet Spot

I'll admit that the poke is the trickiest and riskiest of the five humor tactics, so I'm providing some important do's and don'ts. Read them carefully. Lightly making fun of others can be a great way to bond, but it's all about finding that sweet spot where everyone is laughing together. The best humor for managers is inclusive and leaves everyone feeling good. So the next time you're about to tease a friend or colleague, remember these do's and don'ts—and always keep the laughter light and the love strong. Because in the end, nobody wants to be the punch line.

## Dos and Don'ts

How to do it right:

▼ *Know your audience.* "Ribbing" comes after rapport. If you're in the wrong group, teasing can feel like pouring hot sauce on your Golden Grahams.

▼ *Keep it light.* Stick to quirks and funny habits.
▼ *Positive teasing is like sour candy: It might start with a kick, but it leaves a sweet taste.* If the person you're poking is laughing the hardest, boom—you have struck the right chord.

What to avoid:

▼ *Don't hit below the belt.* Avoid personal insecurities—humor should build up, not body-slam.
▼ *Don't gang up.* Group teasing can turn into bullying faster than a reunion of high school cliques.
▼ *Don't misfire.* A joking jab may be a hit at your BBQ, but it might bomb in your boardroom.

## Take My Advice . . . Please

Let's be honest. Nobody actually wants your advice—or mine. Just ask Socrates. The guy spent his days offering wisdom at no charge. How did that work out for him? They served him poison hemlock for dessert.

If you want people to follow your lead, you've got to be smart about it. This humor tactic can help. Poke some fun. (*But don't put an eye out!*) Make them laugh *first*, and they'll be more open to your suggestions. Whether it's a gentle prod, a little jab, or some light teasing, humor can soften the blow.

Say you are leading a seminar, for example. Instead of sounding like a lecturer—"OK, everybody pay attention"—try something like this:

*"As my cat says, 'Watch closely. I'm only knocking this over once!'"*

Helping a friend let go of the past? Instead of delivering a long monologue, why not try this as an opener:

*"Lynda . . . I have an idea! Let's blame Jim, and you can get on with your life."*

This might make your friend laugh and feel heard at the same time.

Even in an email, this brand of humor can help you make your point. Remember this gem?

*"Proofread your work to make sure you don't words out!"*

Here's a funny message that also gets your message across:

"Don't use too many fonts."

We live in an attention economy. To stand out, your advice has to entertain and engage. Wrap it in a poke joke, and you'll find that not only do people listen, but they may come back for more. Who knew getting a laugh was the key to being taken seriously?

Well, I did. That's why I'm the author.

## The Josh Test

Is poking fun a regular humor tactic for you? If the answer is yes, congratulations: You've tapped into one of the most effective ways to build rapport and strengthen relationships. If not, I suggest lightening up a bit. It's OK to kid around. Josh around with your coworker—especially if his name is actually "Josh."

*If people know you love them, you can roast them!* They'll feel toasted, not burned. This is the key to using humor with others. When done with warmth and affection, a good-natured jab can feel like a compliment. Remember, a little humor can make everything better—yes, even family reunions.

Remember the movie *Joker*? The main character, Arthur Fleck, says, "I used to think that my life was a tragedy, but now I realize it's a comedy."

It's a dark and twisted example, but it highlights a truth: The way we frame our experiences—whether we see them as tragic or humorous—shapes our reality . . . oh, and it can win Oscars.

You'll start worrying a lot less about what people think of you when you remember that they rarely do! Nobody's scrutinizing you as much as you think—they're too busy with their own drama. So why not laugh at yourself? It's the best way to outwit your "critics." And remember, you know the laughter factor strategies while their idea of humor is forwarding cat memes from 2017.

Take the poke pop quiz.

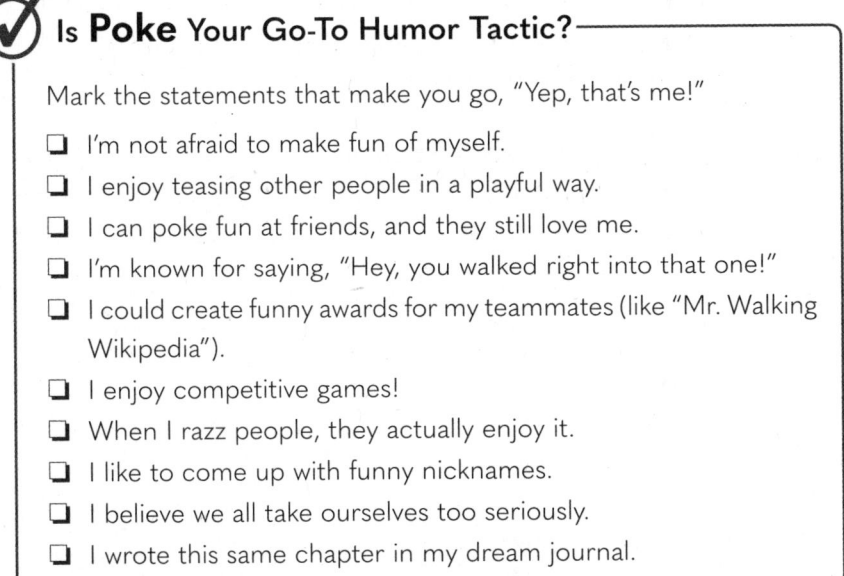

### ✓ Is **Poke** Your Go-To Humor Tactic?

Mark the statements that make you go, "Yep, that's me!"

- ❏ I'm not afraid to make fun of myself.
- ❏ I enjoy teasing other people in a playful way.
- ❏ I can poke fun at friends, and they still love me.
- ❏ I'm known for saying, "Hey, you walked right into that one!"
- ❏ I could create funny awards for my teammates (like "Mr. Walking Wikipedia").
- ❏ I enjoy competitive games!
- ❏ When I razz people, they actually enjoy it.
- ❏ I like to come up with funny nicknames.
- ❏ I believe we all take ourselves too seriously.
- ❏ I wrote this same chapter in my dream journal.

Did you check seven or more of these boxes?

If you see yourself this way, so do other people. And that's good.

The "poking fun" tactic for humor helps you unlock laughter by playfully teasing others. Just keep kindness at the core. Laugh *with* people, not at them. And remember, when you open up and poke fun *at yourself,* you not only break the ice—you melt it. And guess what? People will like you even more.

On your mark, get set, poke!

## Humor Homework

Link: Who in your group geeks out over a team, band, or celebrity? How can you poke some fun at their "idol" in a way that makes them laugh and feel like you get them?

Lift: Do you have a colleague who appreciates a little light roasting? What endearing trait sets them apart? Can you identify and celebrate their one-of-a-kind awesomeness?

Lead: Is there a story you can share about yourself—a funny flop that invites others to laugh at your "failure" while getting to know the real you?

# TACTIC 3

# IN-JOKES

## DISCOVER THE LAUGHTER IN SHARED EXPERIENCES.

A young stand-up comic is invited to lunch at Denny's with a group of longtime comedians. The old pros are so experienced at cracking jokes that they know every single joke ever told. Now they simply call out joke numbers to each other.

Shecky says, "61." They all break up with laughter.

Don shouts out, "27." Everybody howls!

The new guy decides to jump in. "11."

Shocked looks. Dead silence.

Shecky finally says, "Not cool. There are kids here."

With humor tactic 3, poke, we saw how jokes are almost always *on* somebody. But with this humor tactic, it's all about being *in* on the joke. In this chapter, we'll see just how powerful in-jokes can be—and you'll learn how to put them to work for you.

Too often, life can feel like a never-ending group project with people you didn't choose! That's where humor steps in. Laughter isn't just a reaction—it's a *connection hack*. A shared laugh says, "We're in this together." It's the ultimate team-builder and way cheaper than a ropes course.

> **Humor links us best when everyone is in on the joke.**

In the hit comedy TV show *The Office*, lead character Michael Scott said, "I love inside jokes. I'd love to be part of one someday."

Feeling left out of a group is agonizing. It feels like being locked out of a cabin in the freezing cold while your friends are gathered inside around a cozy fireplace. The human heart cries out: *Let me in!*

Humans are naturally tribal. Inside jokes signal who is a member.

Being on the outside of a group's inside humor makes you feel invisible—like you are missing the key to a secret world. But once you are inside, cocreating and cracking those in-jokes, it's like having a "Fast Pass" to feeling connected and vital to your family, friends, team, and clients.

In-jokes are how we say we like each other without being all weird about it.

Ready to experience the fun that comes from fitting in? This four-step sequence lets you into the club.

## Relationships, Remember, Relive, Repeat!

### Relationships

Frank Sullivan, one of America's finest humorists, was known for his contributions to *The New Yorker* magazine. He believed "There is humor that is warming, and tender, and friendly."

When you laugh *with* people, you feel the rush of companionship. Inside jokes are one of life's great pleasures—as long as you are in on the fun. Here's a comment that would be a dud at a comedy club but "crushes" with people in the know at work. "Remember when John 'fixed' the office AC and we all worked in Antarctica for a week?"

In-jokes bloom from relationships. Whether your group meets virtually or in person, it's all about knowing (and surviving!) each other. Common experiences are the fertilizer for funny.

Humor based on shared language and memories unites us. Inside jokes wire and then rewire our hearts . . . *together.* Feel what others are feeling, and the funny follows. When you indulge in shared humor, you rediscover the connections that bind you to other people—those moments of delight that whisper in your ear: *You're part of the family.*

That's when the real magic begins. This type of humor then becomes contagious within your group—like a cold that everybody in your office passes along, but without all the NyQuil. Relationships are what makes in-jokes irresistible because *the people we enjoy the most are the ones we laugh the hardest with.*

In-group humor works like a charm. Of course, these bits won't be funny to people outside your inner circle. Every group sounds strange to those outside it.

But you will "slay" with material that echoes your shared memories with the people you have relationships with. It's easy. Just reflect on *what you have experienced together.* The in-jokes almost write themselves:

▼ *Office:* How about the time Bob tried to fix the printer? It's still in therapy.
▼ *Group photo:* What "group" photo? Jesse sent us a collage of eight selfies.
▼ *Game night:* No more house rules—unless we want to see Steve invent another "Steve wins!" rule.

▼ *Text chain:* Let's see how long it takes before Alex hits us with, "Sorry, I just saw this!" six hours later.

▼ *Reunions:* Let's meet at 8 p.m. PST (and hey, that doesn't stand for Paula's Sense of Time).

▼ *Family trip:* Happy update: This year's vacation doesn't include Dad's shortcut through the wilderness.

## Remember

Inside jokes thrive on shared memories and unique experiences. Remember those moments that brought laughter and camaraderie. These memories become the fuel for in-jokes—whether it's a workplace mishap, a hilarious incident during a presentation, or a memorable group outing. Even a mispronounced word during a team presentation can become an enduring source of amusement. The ability to recall these moments bonds you together and makes the humor authentic and relatable.

> "Hey, remember when Daryl tried to photocopy
> his ham sandwich?"

Shared memories trigger humor that feels like home to your group.

These "remember when" moments activate a secret bond, like a six-digit passcode only your group knows. They're the stories that make your group feel like a tight-knit tribe. You are not just in the same boat—you are on the same wavelength.

*It's almost too easy.*

Picture this: You're in a meeting, and someone brings up a "remember when" moment from the past. Suddenly, the room erupts in laughter, and you can feel the camaraderie skyrocket.

Memory is a funny thing—until you lose it. (My uncle used to say, "I'm great at remembering faces—I just don't know where I put them!")

Our shared history is filled with humor. When you call upon an in-joke with your "inside" group, you are subtly reminding them, *We've been through a lot together*.

And you don't have to rely on one-liners. Just pull up a group memory. It's like throwing pieces of bread into a lake—the ducks are magnetically drawn to it.

Here's a tip for this technique: "Talk shop" that's specifically funny to your people.

Remind your group that it has its own weird lingo—a set of acronyms, sayings, or inside knowledge that only they understand. Shared memories are like built-in punch line generators. For example:

▼ With a tech team, you might say, "Remember when rebooting the server meant yanking the cord? We nearly landed our own 'Unplugged' slot on MTV!"

▼ In a medical office, you might say, "Remember when Dr. Smith 'accidentally' ordered five thousand pairs of latex gloves? We thought we were opening a balloon animal business."

These remembrances are entertaining to insiders only because they are embedded in the shared experiences that everyone in the room relates to. When you bring up these memories intentionally, you're bringing everyone back to a recollection that bonds them together . . . again.

In-jokes make you feel like you have a backstage pass to a private party.

*Saturday Night Live* alum Bill Hader is one of the funniest comedians working today. His hero? Phil Hendrie. This man is the mastermind behind one of the funniest radio and podcast shows ever. Hendrie creates outrageous "fake" characters his audience believes are real people. He pulls listeners into the lives of these personalities. We feel as if we know them! The amazing thing? Hendrie does all the voices himself! How does he do it? Hendrie says, "Comedy comes out of reality." He bases these characters on people he has met.

Some of your best laugh opportunities will come to you the same way Hendrie creates his humor: by relating stories about *particular* people you've met and about the *places* where you have worked.

If you work in the food service industry, try this example:

> I worked as a server. A grouchy regular came into our restaurant and asked, "Do you serve crabs here?" I said, "Sure, take a seat."

Maybe you are a health care professional speaking to colleagues:

> I agree with Erma Bombeck. She said, "Never go to a doctor whose office plants have died."

Or if you are a marriage counselor talking to other marriage counselors:

> "I had a patient who thought monogamy was a board game."

Let's say you are in education, speaking to teachers:

> "One day I asked my class, 'What's a bigger problem today, ignorance or apathy?' A young man raised his hand and answered, 'I don't know. And I don't care!'"

Here's one for pastors to share with fellow ministers about how people aren't always generous givers:

> I was a guest preacher at a church. This congregation had a reputation for not giving. They asked me if I believed in "free speech." When I said "yes," they said, "Good, we'd like you to give one."

> They told me I could pass the hat around after my sermon. I gave my best message that day. When it came time to collect the offering, we

passed the hat. When they brought it forward, I looked inside. There wasn't even a dollar. As I was leaving the church, the organist asked me why I was smiling. I told her,

"Well, at least I got my hat back!"

Even a place you have in common can help you build a bridge. Here's another scenario: You are leading a workshop. All the attendees are staying at the *same hotel*. That's a shared experience. Riff about it:

▼ Does anyone here have a degree in mechanical engineering? I want to figure out how to turn on the shower in my hotel room.
▼ This is a nice clean hotel. At the last place I stayed, they changed the sheets every day . . . from one room to another.
▼ This hotel is amazing. The pillows are so fluffy. I hope I can get my suitcase closed.

## Relive

In their study on humor and group effectiveness, researchers Eric Romero and Anthony Pescosolido document how humor, including inside jokes, contributes to group cohesiveness and productivity. I'm not a scholar. I'm a professional humorist, so let me summarize the study for you in three words: *Funny feels good.*

The essence of inside jokes lies in reliving the merry moments. Share these anecdotes during group gatherings, business meetings, or casual conversations. Quirky client interactions can become hilarious reenactments—*after* your team closes the deal or delivers the goods.

By reliving these experiences, you get some great laughs, and you strengthen the emotional connection within your group.

Comedy = Tragedy + Time

Some of the things we laugh at today seemed awful when they happened. Later, they make for great stories that everyone can relate to because they experienced it, too.

However, keep in mind: *Recollections may vary.*

Ever notice we're all unreliable narrators? That's the fun part. Ask everyone else what *really* happened. Got a teammate who "never" cheats at Jenga? Sure, the tower just *happens* to fall right after Wesley's turn. Joke about it and let him reconstruct his version of the story—one block at a time.

Pro tip: Timing is everything. Jumping the gun on a sad memory by cracking a joke and saying, "Too soon?" is awkward. Let the pain settle before stacking jokes on top of a situation.

## Repeat!

Repetition is key to embedding in-jokes into your friend and work groups. When you continually recall these remarkable stories and memories, something special happens. The nostalgia somehow feels brand-new. It's weird, but it works.

Like that mustard stain on your favorite white shirt, the funny doesn't fade away. With each retelling, those jokes become the "fun fabric" of your group's identity. It's like an imaginary uniform that everyone wants to wear.

One of the big secrets behind the humor tactic of in-jokes is the sneaky brilliance of what comedians call the "callback." Callbacks crack us up because they tap into our love for the familiar—like bumping into an old friend who owes you money but makes you laugh so hard that you forget to ask for it back.

We all have that friend or coworker who tells the same story at every gathering. Somehow, it just gets funnier every time.

"I've heard that one—but please tell it again!"

Repeating stories and certain group sayings adds a dash of spice to a dish we want to relish again. It's in this repetition that the real fun happens. Often, these are catchphrases that, when repeated, create a ripple of laughter that spreads through your group. *Like Tina always says: "Not my circus, not my monkeys."*

We would probably not have Jimmy Fallon, Stephen Colbert, or Jimmy Kimmel had it not been for the late great Jack Benny. He was one of the biggest stars in radio and TV history. He once said, "I don't deserve this award, but I have arthritis, and I don't deserve that, either."

Benny was a master of the callback. Whenever someone teased him about being notoriously stingy, he'd respond with one of his catchphrases: "Now cut that out!" Somehow it got funnier every time he said it.

On its own, not exactly an LOL moment, right? But Benny's genius was in the *repetition*. His audiences started to look forward to it, like waiting for the punch line of a joke you've already heard a million times. Soon, people were repeating it themselves. You, too, can capture a simple phrase that takes on a life of its own with your audience.

Benny wasn't just repeating a line. He was also performing it, making it sound fresh every time, even though the audience knew exactly what was coming. Some fans today will actually recite the jokes along with their favorite comedian—this happens regularly when clean comic Brian Regan performs for his thousands of fans.

When you and your group latch onto a ridiculous catchphrase that no one else likely finds funny, that's what makes it yours.

That's the juice of a great callback—it feels unexpected, even when it's anything but. The familiar is funny. Here's another thing about callbacks—they're like an old pair of slippers. The more you wear them, the more comfortable they get.

Never underestimate the power of a callback. This book stresses the power of play. Don't forget the power of *replay!*

Now that you know how callbacks work, it's time to use them to shake things up. As a leader, here's your chance to create fresh traditions, clever ceremonies, and unforgettable moments at your next meeting, event, or team meeting. The laughter factor is always fun. But it can also make your team feel unforgettable.

Your goal is to turn routines into remarkable moments.

Here's how to mix it up:

▼ *Change the scene.* Ditch the usual locations. Move a meeting to the break room, host a picnic, or try something unexpected. "Remember the time we had our brainstorming session on the roof?"

▼ *Cue the flashbacks.* Ask everyone to share a funny or embarrassing childhood story. You'll spark laughter *and* create new

---

### HUMOR HERO: Karith Foster

Karith is an executive leadership and personal development coach who specializes in diversity engagement, or as she calls it, INVERSITY solutions. Drawing on her background in stand-up and improv, she helps organizations approach inclusion with creativity and fun. Her signature strategy is using humor to foster playful connection while focusing on what we have IN common. Karith shows that humor isn't just for laughs. It is a powerful tool for building understanding and resilience. She reminds her clients, "If you can laugh at it, you can get through it."

**Tips from Karith for inclusive humor:**

▼ Whenever you can, make a game of it! Games aren't just for kids—we're never too old for *fun!*

▼ Adopt the philosophy that you can be perfect or you can be happy. (Spoiler alert—there's no such thing as perfect.)

▼ Life is precious (and short), so laugh at yourself and do not take yourself so seriously.

callback material. "When I was seven, I tried to run away but asked my whole family to come along!"

▼ *Add a timer twist.* Set a timer during a business meeting. When it goes off, the speaker has to wrap up what they are saying in one sentence. The results? Often hilarious. "As I was saying . . . goodbye!"

▼ *Bring back the laughs.* Revisit standout moments from previous gatherings. If someone had a legendary slipup, keep it alive. "Remember when Gene took the wrong freeway and ended up in Arizona?"

▼ *Break the routine.* Add an unexpected twist. Start dinner with dessert, or *end* your meeting with an icebreaker. These shifts can become new traditions. "Who knew giving a prize for the worst driver's license photo would be such a hit?" (Well, I did. That's why I included it.)

When you lead with laughter, you build stronger bonds, foster trust, and create a team that's ready to tackle anything.

Next time you meet, gather *up*. Start a new tradition, revive old laughs, and watch how humor turns your group into a team.

## This Time (and Every Time) It's Personal

I've been on the platform or at the podium thousands of times—talking to everyone from corporate execs to health care pros to nonprofit donors. No matter the audience, whether it's a high-stakes keynote or a lighthearted dinner talk, my goal is always the same: *Make a connection that lasts long after the applause fades.*

Here's my record: Sixty-two comedy presentations in one August. At one point, I did six gigs in a single day. It was exhilarating, exhausting—and surprisingly consistent. The feedback kept rolling in: "It feels like you know us!"

This was and still is one of my big secrets.

Every meeting or event is personal to me. It's their moment, their people, their purpose. My job is to celebrate that, with humor tailored just for them. No cheap shots or dirty jokes—everything is custom-built to resonate with the room.

What most people don't know is that every time I step onstage, it feels brand new. Why? Because it is. A different group, a different agenda, a different mission.

But my approach is always the same: lots of *inside humor*.

To make it happen, I start with three questions.

- ▼ *Who's in the room?* Knowing roles and personalities helps me blend in like part of the team—only funnier.
- ▼ *Who's the most-liked leader?* Playful, positive jokes about this person are like having the group's emotional Wi-Fi password.
- ▼ *What are their shared experiences?* Whether it's a big project or a quirky tradition, these moments are comedy gold.

My favorite compliment? "How long have you worked for us?" That's when I know I've nailed it—when it feels like I've been part of their team all along.

And I don't stop there. If Ethan the CEO is famous for his crazy socks, he'll receive a giant set of stockings from me. And the group laughter will linger long after I'm off to the airport.

This is why I love what I do: creating memories through humor. Here's the best part—you're already "in" with your group! You've got the inside scoop from day one. Use that "intel," and watch the laughter (and connection) grow.

Of the five humor tactics I rely on, using *in-jokes* is my first go-to strategy. Here's why: *It's easy to get people laughing at what they're already laughing about.* (Read that sentence again if you need to.) It's like holding up a mirror, reflecting their image, and then highlighting their special brand of "weirdness." It's my way of saying, "I get the one-of-a-kind culture you've spent years building."

When people see themselves in the humor, they don't just laugh—they bond even more deeply, and they remember the experience long afterward.

So the next time you see me onstage, know this: I'm feeling nervous. But I'm also excited. I know most of the humor is going to go over great *because it's personal*.

And it should be for you—and your team—too.

## Let's Get Engaged

Imagine this situation: I was hosting a national marketing meeting. The "draw speaker," the person everyone was actually waiting to see, was a famous *New York Times* bestselling author. And she was set to go on next. But she wasn't in the meeting room, backstage, or even in the restroom. She was nowhere to be seen . . . or heard. *Gulp*.

Just before I walked up to the stage, ready to introduce our MIA speaker, the meeting coordinator sent me an urgent text.

Stall for 10 min. Speaker on her way.

What would you do?

I walked into the audience with my trusty handheld microphone and started engaging with a few of the attendees. This might sound terrifying, but it wasn't. All I did was invite people to share.

The results were *fun*tastic. The in-jokes started writing themselves!

"Julia, what's been your favorite part of the conference so far?" (She answered, "The free swag Anna gives us when we register!")

"Hey, Robby, what are you looking forward to at this meeting?" (He said, "Seeing my buddy Taylor get a standing ovation after his sales seminar.")

"Hey, Kiersten, what's been your biggest takeaway at our summit?"
(She said, "I discovered that Teri is amazing at karaoke!")

I wasn't going for laughs, but they happened. Because I encouraged participation. Now, it wasn't all fun and games—there were a few serious comments. But the point is, people felt welcome to share and interact. I threw in a few witty comments, and the ten minutes flew by.

The guest speaker arrived, but the attendees seemed bored—until the very end of her keynote. Guess why? She made the end of her speech interactive—and the room lit up all over again!

## You Had to Be There

Don't worry if these in-jokes don't crack up people outside your group. That's where the phrase "You had to be there" comes in—this is about humor that works only within your specific group or arena.

A joke where you had to be there is extra-special to everyone who was.

Here's one that will bring a nod and a smile to a group of thinkers:

The marketing major asks, "How can we sell that?"
The economics major asks, "How can we fund that?"
The philosophy major asks, "Would you like fries with that?"

And one for the science fans:

A statistician: "1, 3, 5, 7. . . . All odd numbers are prime."
A physicist: "Except 9—that's experimental error."
A contractor: "Nine's not prime . . . but for an extra $100, I can make it even."

This kind of humor thrives on knowing your community. It flows from the situations and circumstances that only you and your group can truly appreciate. This stuff is comedy gold with an in-group but turns into fool's gold when you try to explain it to someone else.

Take my friend Jen "the Pen" Wallace, a sharp content creator and editor. At her former company, they used a software program called Jar. When the platform announced it would no longer offer customer support, the company had to transfer all their files to a new system. Chaos ensued. Files were lost, clients were upset, and the team felt super frustrated by the new platform.

Enter Sarah Spencer, a quick-witted company leader, who dubbed the whole disaster "Jarmageddon." The term went viral within their work community, sparking laughter that they couldn't keep a lid on. But unless you were there to witness the file migration mayhem, if you used the term "Jarmageddon" you'd probably just get a shrug and a "Huh?"

Some jokes work for just about everybody. Not these—they're just for your peeps. Because *you had to be there.*

## Who's in the Room?

If you want laughter to die out, force an inside joke. Even though I'm a humor pro, I have fallen into this trap several times.

Most recently, I found myself standing on a stage in front of five hundred real estate agents in Dallas, Texas. I love personalizing my humor for groups like this.

Just before I went on to the platform, one of the attendees pulled me aside and gave me an inside scoop. "Hey, you're the comedian, right? You've got to mention Caleb and how he never sinks a putt on the golf course!"

So, I excitedly wove that bit into my opening remarks. "You guys are closing more deals than Caleb is missing putts!" I expected a big laugh. Instead, I was met with crickets—an awkward, deafening silence. Total buzzkill. Even the guy who suggested it didn't crack a smile.

What went wrong? Well, for starters, Caleb wasn't even in the room!

But the bigger issue was that this audience was a mix of agents from different regions. Only a handful of people knew who Caleb was, and even fewer had ever golfed with him.

Laughter lesson learned: *Humor links us best when everyone is in on the joke.*


## Inside Tracks

At Asheville Club—a coffee, beer, and wine bar in downtown Asheville, North Carolina—you don't just grab a drink; you step into a vibe, a shared moment, a special kind of club.

I was there with my wife when a stranger approached, wide-eyed and grinning, like I was his long-lost best friend. For a moment, I wondered: Mistaken identity, or do I owe this guy money? As he got closer, I braced myself for an unsolicited hug. Then it hit me—like walking into a spiderweb at night—he was staring at the vintage King's X shirt I was wearing.

King's X isn't Taylor Swift. She has over a hundred million Spotify listeners while King's X has fifty thousand. But in that moment, the universe united two of us over a T-shirt.

"Bro, I love King's X!" he said, introducing himself as Josiah. In seconds, we were lost in a world of prog-rock riffs and song titles that sounded like Swahili to everyone else.

"They're the best rock trio in history!" Josiah practically shouted. "What are your top five fave tracks?"

I said, "I love the entire *Gretchen Goes to Nebraska* album."

By the end of the day, we were texting like high schoolers with a crush. That's the power of sharing an inside track. It's a vibe. You're tuned in to the same frequency. And that's the essence of in-jokes: *We* bond over things we have in common.

Creating this "club" vibe makes us feel close and creates comedy moments, too.

**Shows:** You both cried during the *Ted Lasso* finale? Instant bond. "You love *Stranger Things*, too? Come to my house for Thanksgiving!"

**Music:** Whether you bond over obscure indie bands or connect with a team member, you agree: "Nickelback *slaps!*"

**Gen Jokes:** Adulting? My parents were boomers who bought a house when they were twenty-three. I'm thirty-nine and just splurged on . . . oat milk. Living the dream!

**Struggles:** Assembling IKEA furniture? Nothing bonds people like fighting over what *modular* means.

**Frustrations:** Both exhausted by a certain coworker's habits? "Ping me again, Kyle—I dare you."

In-jokes thrive on connection, turning "me" into *we*—and sparking laughter that sticks people together. A shared laugh at work turns coworkers into coconspirators!

## Microfamous

Branding expert Matt Johnson coined a term about the power of becoming a trusted voice inside a very small group: microfamous. Johnson wrote an entire book about the opportunities within these niche networks.

Within a small, devoted circle, we feel like rock stars. The outside world might not know what we are singing or laughing about, but within our group, we are the insiders. That's what makes being in a small, connected group so special—you're part of something unique. We are communicating: "Yo . . . we're in the know."

We feel dialed in.

One thing you'll notice: There's usually an element of "us versus them" that goes unstated but is nearly always part of the subtext of our groups. It's like you're saying, "They can't keep us down!" Once you're on that track with a group, you're all in it together, creating your own little world of shared humor and camaraderie. This sense of exclusivity and shared experience strengthens the bonds within the group, making every inside joke and shared laugh even more meaningful.

It feels good to be in the know, to share those winks and nods that make you feel like you're part of something special. So the next time you find yourself bonding over a shared love of something obscure, remember that it's not just about what you know—it's also about who you share it with.

And if all else fails, just throw on a band T-shirt and wait for your tribe to find you. Because in the world of inside tracks, you never know when you're about to meet your next best friend—or create your next inside joke—over a shared experience and a cult-classic riff.

Oh, back to the King's X story for a moment. (I can't stop!) Remember the name of that coffee shop I mentioned where I became fast friends with Josiah? It's Asheville *Club*. That's fitting. Whenever we share the feeling of being on an inside track with others, it makes us feel like we are in a private club. And that's where the best in-jokes begin to flow freely.

## It's All in the Game

There are many funny board games you can purchase and play. Balderdash is a favorite of mine (more on that in tactic 4, wordplay).

For enjoying in-jokes, I recommend you pick up this game: Hot Seat: The Game That's All About You.

Hot Seat is a hilarious way to discover what your friends or coworkers *really* think about you. One person sits in the hot seat and writes down their own answer to a personal question. Everyone else tries to guess their answer.

Fun breaks forth!

This game generates lots of laughs and insider humor with questions like these:

- ▼ My face is on the cover of a cereal box. What is the slogan?
- ▼ What instructional YouTube video would I be famous for?
- ▼ What should be my new nickname?

In a business or corporate setting, Hot Seat is a fun icebreaker or team-building activity. To keep it HR-friendly, simply preselect cards from the question deck and leave out any that are risqué.

Focus on fun, lighthearted topics. If someone in your group gets a card they don't want to answer, they can opt out. That's funny, too!

## Your Presence Is Requested

When you invite a friend to your birthday party, what are you really hoping for? Usually it's two things: their RSVP and their presence (and if you're lucky, their presents).

We hear it all the time: Be present. But you can double that: Be present—and feel *their* presence, too.

This is at the heart of the laughter factor. It's not, "Hey, everybody, I'm funny." It's "We're having a great time together."

So how do you stir up this fun, even if you're not cracking jokes nonstop? The answer is one word: *participation.*

Magicians say, "For my next trick, I'll need a volunteer." Everyone freezes. Don't use that line. But the idea behind it is gold: "Let's experience something wonderful together." Nobody wants to feel "volun-told," but everyone wants to feel included.

Laughter feels amazing when we're not just spectators but participants. Humor is about drawing people in—making them feel like they're part of what's happening, not just watching it.

When I'm onstage, I weave interactive bits into my talks. I don't care if someone in the audience gets more laughs than I do, as long as everybody's laughing. You can do this too, without mastering sleight of hand (or sleight of mouth). Just remember these three "I" actions:

**I will . . .**
**. . . make my humor inviting.**

Use humor like a welcome mat. "You're here! Come on in. Take your shoes off . . . unless your socks stink." Be conversational and approachable. Let people feel in on the joke, not the butt of it. The goal is *always* connection, not showing off.

**. . . make my humor interactive.**

Encourage participation! Go beyond "Raise your hand if. . . ." This isn't a live auction. Instead, create a back-and-forth flow. Mention names, give people something to do, and make them feel part of the action. Engaged people don't just listen—they live the moment with you.

**. . . make my fun inclusive.**

Involve everyone, and you can't bore them. When people are part of the experience, they're naturally entertained (or at least too involved to be checking their Insta).

Remember, your goal is not to be the funniest person in the room; it's to make others feel part of something special. Get them involved, get them laughing, and watch as your relationships deepen. If you do it right, no one will be on their phone, secretly refreshing their fantasy football stats.

Take this amusing assessment.

Are **In-Jokes** Your Go-To Humor Tactic?

Do you recognize yourself in these statements?

- ❏ I thrive on inside jokes that make "outsiders" go, "Wait, what?"
- ❏ My group chat is 70 percent jokes only we get.
- ❏ I love to talk to friends in our special code.
- ❏ My coworkers always want me to "Tell that story about when. . . ."
- ❏ I sprinkle "callbacks" into conversations.
- ❏ For me, there's nothing better than connecting over a shared experience.
- ❏ Improv games? Sounds fun to me!
- ❏ Secret handshakes, funny traditions—I'm all in.
- ❏ I like to explain our "house rules" for games with friends.
- ❏ People often ask me to "spill the tea."
- ❏ Who's King's X? Let's talk about Chappell Roan!

If you checked seven or more of these boxes, welcome to the club.

In-jokes deepen bonds by reliving shared experiences and cracking us up with "code" language.

In-jokes make your connections deeper . . . and funnier.

## Humor Homework

**Link:** What shared memory can you turn into a funny inside joke that deepens your team's connection? How can you bring *everyone* into the story to strengthen those bonds?

**Lift:** Spark a laugh today that energizes and empowers your team. What moment can you relive together to remind them "We got this"?

**Lead:** What playful twist can you add to your talk to inspire and unite? Can you create a quirky catchphrase, a lighthearted challenge, or a new tradition to celebrate your team? How will you make it fun, inspiring, and unmistakably "ours"?

# WORDPLAY

## USE WITTY **LANGUAGE** AND CLEVER BANTER.

The pope dies and goes to heaven. Saint Peter is overjoyed to see him. He tells the pope, "I was the first pope. I am so glad you are in heaven with us. What is the first thing I can show you here in paradise?"

The pope says, "Do you have the original Bible?"

Saint Peter says, "Yes. We have the very first handwritten copy. Let me get it for you." He leads the pope to a special waiting room.

A few minutes later he brings the pope the very first copy of the Bible and tells him, "Enjoy! I will be back in an hour to check on you." But when Saint Peter returns an hour later, the pope is weeping, with his finger on *one* word of the text.

Saint Peter says, "What's wrong?"

The pope says, "The word was cele-*brate*!"

Get it? Sometimes I tell that joke onstage. Half the audience laughs, and the other half pretends to get it—which is also funny.

If you enjoy word*play* and don't mind some people wanting to throw things at you, you'll love this humor tactic. If you love punch lines, puns, and pithy sayings, you've come to the *write* place. In this chapter, I offer a wealth of examples. Sure, you'll groan, but you will also grin. You'll find tips for flexing this laugh language, plus inspiration for building your own wordplay vocabulary.

Chances are the first joke you learned as a kid was a knock-knock joke. Remember those? They were created before we had TikTok dance clips. It's based on a wonderful premise: Somebody is knocking at your door. The punch lines are puns that riff on the word *who*.

Knock, knock.
Who's there?
Boo.
Boo who?
Well, you don't have to cry about it!

## What Are Words Worth?

Use your sense of humor to make people laugh, not cry. They say talk is cheap, but it's really not if it costs you your job or a meaningful relationship. Cutting words can be costly. Try asking your mom if her Christmas dessert came from the microwave. You might get served a cold dish of hot apple pie right to the forehead. Ask any business leader who's had to step down after using inappropriate language at work.

The goal here is to use language to link, lift, and lead. Oh, and to make 'em laugh!

Words pack a punch, but you can serve them up like punch and cookies. The right words can light up—or at least lighten up—a room. Clever words can even turn a dull conversation around. And here's the best part: Playing with words can make you more winsome—*if* you don't overdo it. The goal isn't to monopolize with wordplay. If you do that, you won't advance to Go or collect $200.

Language isn't just a strategy—it's the field of play. Soccer legend Henrikh Mkhitaryan said, "Tactics are just small details that show you the way to play." This humor tactic works the same way—small, clever twists of language can make communication more enjoyable, whether with colleagues, friends, or kids who have no idea what you're talking about.

## Word Bonds Make Friendships More Fun

Wordplay in friendships adds that little something extra. Instead of "Let's grab coffee," try "Let's espresso ourselves!" A tiny tweak can tickle and create a new catchphrase you both love to repeat.

Take the men's groups that meet to talk about life, theology, and fatherhood. They smoke cigars together. When they named their gatherings "Holy Smokes," the idea caught fire—literally. No joke. Google it. Now men worldwide puff each other up around this clever name.

## Words at Work

In business, wordplay can set a playful tone. Drafting a "No Remote" work policy? Start with, "Don't try this at home . . ."

Three quick puns for workplace announcements:

▼ *Monday Book Club:* "We're reading a book about antigravity—it's impossible to put down."
▼ *Wednesday Cookie Club:* "Join us . . . if you have the dough."
▼ *Fitness Friday:* "Come for kettlebells, stay for cocktails."

## Wordplay at Home

Are you a parent? Remember the silly rhymes from childhood. "Fuzzy Wuzzy was a bear. Fuzzy Wuzzy had no hair!" (Poor Fuzzy suffered from bear pattern baldness.) You can pay that fun forward with your kids. Instead of saying, "It's healthy snack time," try saying, "It's orange o'clock!" Or ask, "Who wants ice cream?" And when they answer "Me," you reply with a scream, "*Aaaaagggghhhh!*"

# Silver Linings

So, what are words worth? More than you may think. Playful language sparks laughter, strengthens connections, and brings people together. Whether you're turning routines into mini-adventures, building friendships, or making work communications pop, wordplay is a tool worth using.

> I insulted my friend Terry, and now I feel awful.
> My doctor says I'm suffering from dissin' terry.

If you ever doubt the power of a pun like this, remember that a book titled *The Pun Also Rises: How the Humble Pun Revolutionized Language, Changed History, and Made Wordplay More Than Some Antics* became a runaway bestseller. The author, John Pollack, was invited to speak at Google headquarters. (I'm sure he is jealous of my weeklong run at Waffle House.)

Before we move forward with these "light sentences," let's take a quick look back.

# Who Was Al Boasberg?

Al "the Gag Man" Boasberg was one of the best comedy writers in American history. He wrote laughable lines for some of the most famous funny men and women of the twentieth century, including Groucho Marx, Bob Hope, and many others. In a moment, I'll show you how he can help you with humor today.

Boasberg was *not* a professional comedian himself. He was once cast in a musical called *Love in the Suburbs*. His acting was so bad the producer told him, "If you quit, I'll double your salary!"

But at one point, Boasberg was getting paid handsomely to write jokes for 150 comedians. Before the late, great Jack Benny died, he offered Boasberg a golden contract—a million dollars a year in today's money—to write clever bits for him.

What was the Gag Man's secret?

*Words.*

He never attended college, but he loved words. Playing with language was his secret key to creating funny lines. He told friends, "I own two books: a dictionary and a thesaurus."

The Gag Man said something else that can help sharpen your sense of humor:

"I write with my ears."

Things that *sound* funny to you will help generate laughter in just about any setting. Using this humor tactic will enhance your ability to make an impact as a speaker, manager, or group leader. In fact, wordplay can boost you in any role where you want to sound remarkable.

Let's explore this language of laughter and some creative ways to incorporate "clever" into our communication.

## Be Remark-able

Mary Oliver penned over twenty-five books of poetry, but she was not super well known until just one remarkable question she asked went viral: "Tell me, what is it you plan to do with your one wild and precious life?"

What makes a line memorable?

▼ *It's short and to the point:* A great remark is brief. The best ones are sparked by what's happening in the room. Inject a bite-sized line that fits the moment. Maybe you are at the office, and someone asks: "How's the new policy look to you?" You say, "Oh, it's a quick read—like the IRS tax code."

▼ *It's stressed for emphasis:* A great line should be delivered with crisp conviction—even if it sounds like you're saying it off the top of your head. Think of memorable ads, like this one from State Farm: "We know a thing or two, because we've seen a thing or two."

▼ *It's startling:* The reaction you want is, "How did she come up with *that*?" A great line should feel spontaneous and well-timed (even if you've used it before in another setting).

▼ *It's repeatable:* The best remarks are the ones people can't help but repeat. They resonate so well that they spread like bad news at a church social. When I am emceeing an event, here's one I use that people later repeat back to me. After an amazing video or speech, I will say: "WOW! I'll say it backwards . . . WOW!"

## Roll Off Your Tongue

Create a cheat sheet of your favorite laugh lines. Drop these lines into conversations at work and at home. Spice up your emails, texts, and social media posts. You'll start to see (and hear) what resonates. Don't guess. Test.

Collect your favorite laugh lines. Dig deeper than a quick Google search. Purchase a handful of wise and witty quotation books. One of my favorites is *Short Flights: Thirty-Two Modern Writers Share Aphorisms of Insight, Inspiration, and Wit,* compiled by James Lough and Alex Stein. My all-time fave might be Robert Byrne's *The 2,548 Wittiest Things Anybody Ever Said.*

You'll find gems like this one by Leo Roberts: "If life gives you lemons, squirt the juice in people's eyes."

Keep a joke book in your bathroom. What makes you laugh is likely to make other people do the same. Look for the right situations to sprinkle in these smile-makers. When the moment is right, let your funny fly.

But, ah, when is the right moment? One of the key comedy rules of the laughter factor is:

*Timing is everything.*

Don't force humor into moments that don't call for it. Saying, "Hey, I've got a joke for you—it's your new salary," is probably ill-advised if you are a hiring manager.

Here are some examples of funny quips for group settings:

▼ When I am hosting an event and we have been having meals throughout the gathering, I dismiss the attendees by saying, "Until we eat again . . ."
▼ After an amazing musical performance: "And imagine what he'll sound like when he goes *full-time!*"
▼ Announcing start times: "Please be on time. Last night I asked the front desk for a *wake-up call.* The guy said, 'Wake-up call? Are you sure? OK. You're overweight and you need a new haircut.'"

Let me give you a pro tip on how to deliver lines like this.

## Don't Call Me Shirley

Siri kept calling me "Shirley" today. Maybe because I left my phone on *Airplane* mode.

Recognize the source for this one? Leslie Nielsen was a master of deadpan humor. In that famous movie scene, his stern response to "Surely you can't be serious" was, "I am serious . . . and don't call me Shirley."

You can use this technique to get laughs like Leslie did. Deliver your funny line like it's a matter of national security—seriously. Keep a very straight face.

Do not laugh at your own joke or funny story. Wait . . . for them to laugh. Punch up your punch line and pause for effect.

To be funny, you don't have to be silly.

*Our love of funny language is actually hardwired into our brains.*

Play. It. Straight.

The following word for clever quips is super cool. Get ready for . . .

## Zingers!

My favorite word to describe these short quips has also been applied to a tasty treat made by Hostess Brands. *Zingers* add impact to whatever you are saying.

Imagine you are hosting a group meeting and saying hello to new members:

"Welcome to our team. We put the fun in dysfunctional."

These short attention-grabbers make you sound witty—and you will be when you inject a jolt of light that brightens your speech, sales presentation, sermon, or story.

Zingers are powerful because they *pop*. So you'll want to limit using them to moments when you want to emphasize some-thing. Think of them like exclamation marks. Use sparingly ! (I'm a hypocrite ! ! ! ! ! !)

When overused, zingers can derail a conversation or trivialize what others are saying. Use them like pepper, not like salt or ketchup.

For maximum impact, deliver your zinger with zest. Take a breath before you drop your phrase. Then pause a beat *after* you say it. *Kaboom.* You'll get a nice laugh.

Hosting a sales award meeting? Maybe you want to kick things off with a zinger:

"Tonight we recognize our top achievers. As Zig Ziglar once said, 'Unassertive salespeople have skinny kids.'"

You are giving a motivational talk:

"Always give 100 percent . . . unless you're donating blood."

These are like mini mic-drop moments. They pack a punch. And though they seem spontaneous, zingers require preparation.

Here's an example. Concerns about aging politicians are not new to our time. When Ronald Reagan was questioned about his age and his ability to govern, he used a zinger against his opponent, Walter Mondale:

"I will not make age an issue. I will not exploit my opponent's relative youth and inexperience."

Some historians think he may have won the presidency with this single line!

Find (or create) a favorite funny line to bring some zing to your next talk.

## Spinning Words

I've had many public performances go wrong—*way* wrong. One time, I accidentally lit a stage on fire and set off a fire alarm. Another time, I introduced a famous musician by the wrong name (he shall remain nameless here, to protect . . . me).

But my favorite time ever in front of an audience was at my high school talent show when I posed as a lead singer. I felt like Harry Styles—without the style. What made it especially meaningful to me? My dad was in the audience.

What gave me the confidence to rock that high school cafeteria auditorium? I took something *known*, something popular at that time, and with my buddy Mark "Clowie" Cloward—whom I've known since fourth grade—we turned it into a hilarious song that rocked the house.

Even though I grew up in the era of "Say no to drugs," a very popular hit at that time was "Cocaine" by Eric Clapton. We knew everyone loved the tune. We changed up the words. Here's a sample of our lyrical prowess:

> If you're in the mood for some Chinese food, chow mein
> If you don't want to show, why don't you order to go,
>
> Chow mein
> Comes with rice, comes with rice, comes with rice . . .
> Chow mein!

OK, maybe you had to be there. But I *was* there, and the young crowd was into it. Why? Because we took a song they knew and had a ton of fun changing the words around. You can do the same thing—no drug references required!

Take words people know and give them your spin with wordplay. If you're a financial advisor, you could insert this into your pitch:

> "You may not come from a wealthy family—but a wealthy family can come from you!"

Let's say you're a personal development coach, wanting your clients to remember the importance of verbal declarations:

"What you *say* is what you *get*."

Or maybe you're leading a financial project, encouraging your team to unite around a targeted goal, without losing money:

"We're all in the same boat—let's make sure no one's drilling holes in it!"

The point is, repeat a familiar phrase, song, or cliché, and give it a playful twist. And this technique is not just for the stage, boardroom, or classroom—language is the game room in the house of humor.

## Quick Hits of Humor

Here's how to successfully land verbal zingers:

- ▼ *Keep them short:* Great one-liners pack a mighty punch. The setup is what's happening; the punch is your twist. Done.
- ▼ *Find the moment:* Don't shove your joke into a conversation like you are pitching a multi-level marketing biz. But have a few gems ready (hello, iPhone notes). Drop your line when it fits.
- ▼ *Make it pop:* The best quips have a surprising edge. They sound timeless. Will Rogers said this (and he died way back in 1935): "A fool and his money are soon elected."
- ▼ *Match the vibe:* A great line should make people think, *How'd they come up with that so fast?* Even if it's planned, it should feel as fresh as guac at your bachelorette party.
- ▼ *Refine your go-tos:* Many great lines are polished over time. Discover your favorites and tweak them. Write something you think is funny. Then ask a friend (even if your friend's name is "ChatGPT"), "How can I make this *funnier*?"

▼ *Abbreviate:*

> Simplify, simplify!
>
> *—Henry David Thoreau*

> Simplify!
>
> *—Samuel Patrick Smith*

## Rhyme Time

Remember when short, catchy rhymes used to delight you and your friends?

*They still can.*

We are all kids at heart. In today's world of information overload, rhyming phrases equal smiling faces.

Insert short rhymes into your presentations or conversations. Make your messages more memorable by adding this touch of fun to the mix.

For instance, when you need to emphasize confidentiality, why settle for the plain old "Hey, everybody, this stays with us, OK?" Instead, say:

"Zip it, lock it, put it in your pocket."

It's a playful way to make the same point—and you may not have to email legal.

Create rhymes to fit your roles and whoever it is you're addressing. You can borrow these examples, which I came up with for you:

▼ *Salespeople:* "All aboard, full reward."
▼ *Content creators:* "Viral trick, record it quick!"
▼ *Your kids:* "If you'll play fair, we'll go somewhere."

▼ *Theater people:* "Off the page and onto the stage."
▼ *Comics being coached:* "Write it down, or you'll always be a birthday clown."
▼ *Poker players:* "3-bet, C-bet." (Know what that means? You betcha.)

Short rhymes can go viral within your group. Pick a few you love, but not too many. Your pleasure may not be their treasure.

## Sounds Like Fun

Ever notice how a smell can transport you somewhere else? Sounds do much the same thing for our brains—they can trigger laughter and send your people straight to Ha Ha Land.

I'm not suggesting you slip a whoopee cushion onto your boss's chair. Funny? Sure. A smart move before a quarterly review? Not so much. Instead, focus on language that *sounds* humorous. Wildly descriptive words tickle our ears.

Take "gargantuan"—a word that has to squeeze through the door sideways. Or "flabbergasted"—it sounds like the noise you'd make seeing your ex ride a llama into your house. Silly-sounding words like "mumbo jumbo" or "straight-up wackadoo" can turn ordinary descriptions into laugh-out-loud moments.

Wordplay isn't just about clever phrases; it's about the sounds—like a rubber chicken slap. Rhythm, repetition, and how words bounce off the tongue to create verbal jazz that keeps people hooked.

One of my favorite words? *Superfluous* (su-PER-flew-us). If you don't know it, look it up. It's a word that contradicts itself—like a looooong lecture about the importance of brevity.

Try this: Next time you're chatting or emailing, add some sound effects. Sprinkle in alliteration, rhyming, or a word that's just plain fun to share. It'll make people laugh and your message stick.

## HUMOR HERO: Dr. Mardy Grothe

A psychologist and lifelong quotation collector, Dr. Mardy Grothe has authored numerous books on wit and wordplay, including *Metaphors Be with You* and *Viva la Repartee*. Mardy believes that "the best laughter is inspired by wit." And he reminds us: "Words have incredible power. They can make people's hearts soar, or they can make people's hearts sore."

**Mardy's tips for using language for laughter:**

▼ Instead of trying to be a great wit yourself, which can fall flat or backfire, have a stockpile of witty quotations ready to insert into a conversation.

▼ Draw on metaphorical quotes. Lynda Barry said, "Love is an exploding cigar we willingly smoke." Paint word pictures: "Don't let a fool kiss you, or a kiss fool you."

▼ Study great retorts, like Jennifer Lopez's answer when asked what she got on her SAT score: "Nail polish."

▼ A good sense of humor depends far less on what you *say* than on what you *see*.

In tactic 5, amplify, we'll explore how tone, volume, and inflection can make you sound even funnier.

## May I Have a Word with You?

Our love of funny language is actually hardwired into our brains, and making others laugh with just one word comes naturally to us. Sometimes, when it comes to sharing our sense of humor, we mistakenly think we have to become zany or silly or embarrass ourselves. This is not the case, especially with language-based laughter. A single word can do the trick!

*The Princess Bride* has become a classic comedy loved by millions around the world. Are you a fan of this film? Most people I know love it. In fact, I have friends who love to quote lines from the movie all the time.

This movie is more about wordplay than swordplay. One of my favorite parts of the film is how the grumpy character Vizzini keeps repeating the word "inconceivable!" It gets me every time.

You can create laugh lines by emphasizing just one word in a sentence. Notice how in these examples, the laugh comes from the punch of just one word:

▼ Back to Steven Wright, a master of wordplay, who says, "When I was a little kid, we had a sandbox. It was a quicksand box. I was an only child . . . *eventually.*"

▼ Speaking of kids, here's one from a children's joke book: "I lost my job at the orange juice factory. . . . I couldn't *concentrate.*"

▼ "My mom told me marriage is a three-ring circus: the engagement ring. The wedding ring. The *suffering.*"

Are there words you like to repeat? Choose them carefully and emphasize them for effect. Sometimes it's not just the word, but the way you say it. I've shared the following joke with educators, and they love it. By emphasizing one letter of a word, it gets a nice laugh:

My parents were on a flight to Hawaii for their anniversary. Everything was fine until they got into an argument about how you pronounce the word "Hawaii." My mom was insistent: "Honey, the way you say the word is Ha-vie-ee." My dad told her, "No. You just say it

with the W. The state is pronounced 'Ha-why-ee.'" Back and forth
they went. My mom said, "No, it's 'Ha-vie-ee.'" My dad was adamant:
"It's just 'Ha-why-ee.'"

Finally, to win the argument, my mom tapped the shoulder of the
older gentleman seated in front of them.

"Excuse me, sir. Can I get your opinion? My husband says we are head-
ing to Ha-why-ee. I say the name of the state is pronounced Ha-vie-
ee. What do you say?"

The man answered her immediately. "It's pronounced Ha-vie-ee."

My mom said, "I knew it! Thank you very much, sir."

And he said, "You're velcome."

## Dad Jokes Are Apparent

Why are dad jokes so popular?

In today's world, dad jokes have become the fast food of funny—
they are quick and easy to tell, and they're guaranteed to get a
reaction.

Dad jokes make us feel at ease. That's why they aren't called "weird
uncle jokes." They're a playful way to lighten the mood and spread a
bit of joy without ruffling any feathers.

These little gems are loved for their simple, clever wordplay, and
the nostalgic feeling they evoke. Dad jokes make family gatherings
(and corporate meetings) a lot more fun.

Exchanging puns links us with laughter. These jokes bridge gener-
ation gaps and get everyone chuckling—or at least rolling their eyes—
together. Dad jokes are also great for moms, daughters, grandkids,
and your work family.

Whether it's an old favorite or a new groaner, these jokes connect us with shared humor, because we nearly always react to them. It's the fun of wordplay. Consider these classics:

I went to a concert for just 45 cents. It featured 50 Cent and Nickelback.

Never buy anything made of Velcro. It's a total rip-off.

And who doesn't love:

Did you hear about the guy who invented Life Savers? He made a mint.

The list goes on . . .

I used to play piano by ear, but now I use my hands.

Even when they elicit a groan, puns remind us that sometimes the silliest jokes can garner the biggest *reactions*. But don't overdo it. Getting pelted with fruit is also a reaction.

Take a lesson from the best Scrabble players. The purpose of wordplay is to score points. In the right setting, puns do this for you—they score with your audience. Have fun with them. But use them in moderation. The last thing you want is for people to send you to a *pun*itentiary.

Speaking of punishment . . .

## Sarcasm Is My Superpower

If you're anything like me, sarcasm is one of your most tempting wordplay tactics. It's that sharp, witty way of saying the *opposite* of what you mean. It's pure heaven! And it *can* get lots of laughs from those around you.

Think of it as positive humor's rebellious cousin.

Saying the opposite of what you mean is a fast way to be funny. When it's blistering hot inside, you say, "I just *love* our new air-conditioning unit." You are with a coworker in bumper-to-bumper traffic. You smile and say, "They'll be so impressed when we get there early."

Sarcastic humor has bite:

▼ If you break your leg, don't come running to me.

▼ I have been reading about how bad drinking is. So I stopped . . . reading.

▼ I went up to a clerk at a clothing store. "Hi. Do you work here?" She said, "No, I'm an employee."

Sarcasm can be hilarious, but it needs to come with a *warning label* (on social media, that's <sarcasm>).

It's funny and appreciated when applied to yourself: *If I could choose* **one** *word to describe myself, it would be: "Doesn't follow directions."*

And it can be funny and *not* appreciated when aimed at others:

▼ I'd like to help you out . . . which way did you come in?

▼ Oh, you have an idea? Let me drop everything and take notes.

▼ I heard that you love long walks. Please take one.

There are entire—quite funny—books on the topic of sarcasm. This is not one of them. Why? This type of cutting humor is not one of our main humor tactics.

Why not?

Wielding sarcasm can make you come across as superior-sounding rather than approachable. Sarcasm often feels like a put-down. And honestly, it's just not everyone's cup of tea. You might end up alienating people when you want to bond with them.

Of course, there are exceptions. Sometimes, with your inside group, sarcasm hits just the right note. But when you're tempted to let it rip, consider passing.

You can get big laughs without belittling.

## Sit-Down Comedy

Who says you have to perform stand-up to create comedy?

Some of the biggest laughs I ever enjoyed happened while playing the board game Balderdash. (The game used to be called Fictionary.) I've played it with family, friends, and even clients. It's a riot. In this game, you craft fake definitions for obscure words and attempt to fool your friends into picking your definition. It's a hilarious mix of wordplay, bluffing, and making your opponents laugh so hard, they fall out of their chairs.

Let's say you draw the card for this word:

"**spline** (n.): a long, flexible strip of wood or the like, used in drawing curves."

Your funny definition—that might fool your friends—could be:

"*spline* (v.): When you ask someone to say what they mean."

Some words can be funny all by themselves. Just say them. Then "riff" on the meanings.

- ▼ *Dramamine:* That describes my high school theater teacher!
- ▼ *Abbreviation:* Why is that such a long word?
- ▼ *Queue:* A line where the "ue" just stands there doing nothing.

As a young man, when I would enter a room, my dad would ask, "What's the good word?" You can also get a nice laugh using the classic good news/bad news formula. This was my dad's favorite joke:

**DOCTOR:** I have good news and bad news. The bad news is, we need to amputate your feet.

**PATIENT:** That's terrible. What's the good news?

**DOCTOR:** The patient in the next bed says he wants to buy your slippers.

Speaking of doctors. . . . A man loses three fingers in a work accident. He asks the doctor, "Can I drive with this hand?" The doctor tells him, "Maybe. But I wouldn't count on it."

## Be a Curious Bird

We're all glad to stop talking about COVID. During the pandemic, I sanitized my hand so much, I found the answers to my eighth-grade Spanish quiz!

But I do want you to experience *corvid*. Let me explain. Embracing corvid means adopting the clever, resourceful nature of the *magpie*, a member of the corvid family. Magpies are curious birds. They collect shiny and interesting objects and pull these pieces together to create something special.

Capture your own collection of funny bits, jokes, and stories. *First, get it in writing.* Use a notebook or your notes app to jot down humor from books, shows, speeches, and funny memes. I have a super-cool 007 Dango wallet that holds my credit cards and has a mini-journal with a secret pen! I jot down anything that makes me laugh. At the end of the month, I transfer the best gems into my laptop and replace the journal with a fresh one. This way, I don't have to keep everything in my head.

Before Robin Williams went onstage, he would review his big folder of favorite jokes and bits of business. He drew on this treasure trove to deliver "spontaneous moments." You'll draw inspiration from unexpected sources—sales reps, customers, kids, and others. Sprinkle some of this humor into meetings, presentations, speeches, and texts.

Once you've gathered your "nest of nuttiness," use the magpie approach to add humor to any situation. Be ready to draw on your jokes to brighten conversations. Practice mixing elements from your humor bank to respond with spontaneity and wit.

Go ahead and catch corvid. Embrace your inner magpie and start collecting—and sharing—your favorite comic bits and pieces. If you feel you are too serious to carry a joke journal, lighten up. Even logic can take a twisted turn:

> All men are mortal.
>
> Socrates is a man.
>
> Therefore, Socrates is mortal.
>
> *OK, then*...
>
> Love is blind.
>
> Marriage is an institution.
>
> So, marriage is an institution for the blind.

Laughter follows logically from wacky wordplay. To illustrate, here's one of my all-time favorite jokes by Ronnie Shakes:

> After twelve years of therapy, my psychiatrist said something that brought tears to my eyes. He said, *"No hablo inglés."*

## Humorous Headlines

Is your organization making news? Before you launch into those exciting updates, you can say, "Hey, our team's news beats some of the local headlines I have been reading about nationwide."

As you look at your phone, read off a few of these "news updates":

▼ "Employee falls through roof into marijuana storage unit. He says: 'The deeper I went, the higher I got.'"

▼ "College prevents student protests by calling them required courses."

▼ "Man admitted to hospital. Twenty-two plastic horses found in his stomach. Doctors say his condition is stable."

Or maybe one of these actual headlines from *The Onion*:

▼ World Death Rate Holding Steady at 100 Percent.
▼ CIA Realizes It's Been Using Black Highlighters All These Years.
▼ Winner Reveals He Didn't Even Know It Was Pie-Eating Contest.

Your group may not die laughing, but humorous headlines are a funny way to frame your talk. Hey, speaking of everybody's favorite humor topic, death . . .

## At Wits' End

We are mere mortals. But some people leave us . . . laughing. Believe it or not, I've officiated at a number of memorial services, and several people have asked me, "Can you put some fun into the funeral?"

While it might seem inappropriate, it's not. When we lose a loved one, we need to experience both sadness and joy. Humor helps us heal. Canadian comedian Dave Madden said, "My uncle's funeral cost $5,000 so far. We buried him in a rented tuxedo."

Henriette Mantel said, "If I am ever stuck on a respirator or a life-support system, I definitely want to be unplugged—but not till I get down to a size 8."

Here's one more I love:

The man who invented the word search died.
His funeral will be held next . . .

| T | T | I | S | P | V | G | K | M |
|---|---|---|---|---|---|---|---|---|
| H | J | G | U | O | N | Q | U | X |
| N | M | O | N | D | A | Y | W | Z |
| B | A | T | K | T | E | N | O | P |
| H | C | V | N | K | O | T | D | I |

I know, I know—this is a grave matter. (Sorry!) But even our final statements can be funny . . . with the wit of wordplay. Who says you can't leave 'em laughing?

"Remember, if you don't go to other people's funerals, they won't come to yours."

How about some hilarious headstones?

Here Lies John Yeast: Pardon Me for Not Rising

Here Lies the Body of Jonathan Blake:

Stepped on the Gas Instead of the Brake

The Shell Is Here, but the Nut Is Gone

*—June M. Wingo (1948–2005)*

There Goes the Neighborhood

*—Rodney Dangerfield (1921–2004)*

I Told You I Was Sick

*—Spike Milligan (1918–2002)*

Keep the Line Moving

*—Jack Paar (1918–2004)*

And a few more from some others who exited with a mic drop:

I Was an Atheist: All Dressed Up and No Place to Go

I Was Hoping for a Pyramid

Now I Know Something You Don't

## Laugh after Death

No joke, one time I was hired to entertain an association of morticians. I thought it would be a terrible gig. I was wrong. Though I avoided "dead jokes" that night, *they* didn't. They understand that life is short, and we must live it up while we can. (Some of these funeral directors—no kidding—said things to me like, "Man, you really killed this crowd.")

Speaking of funerals, let's talk about one of the most unforgettable moments in television history—a scene that still makes people laugh, years later.

Decades before Tina Fey became a TV star, Mary Tyler Moore was one of the most loved—and influential—people in the history of television. "MTM" had a singular gift for bringing humor to life. She didn't just star in a sitcom; she turned it into a cultural phenomenon. Mary Tyler Moore died in 2017, but the smiles and laughter she brought us live on.

One of her most iconic moments came in an episode of *The Mary Tyler Moore Show* titled "Chuckles Bites the Dust." It's been called one of the funniest episodes in TV history. The plot centers around Mary and her coworkers attending the funeral of a beloved television character, Chuckles the Clown.

The minister's somber eulogy for "Chuckles" perfectly captures the humorous heart of *The Mary Tyler Moore Show*—and reminds us of the joy of wordplay.

Talking about how Chuckles brought laughter to the world and didn't expect much in return, the minister says, "A little song, a little dance, a little seltzer down your pants."

The gold of this episode was watching Mary struggle valiantly to suppress her laughter during this eulogy—and finally fail. You must find this clip on YouTube!

The theme song to *The Mary Tyler Moore Show* refers to how she "could turn the world on with her smile." Her husband of thirty-three years, cardiologist Dr. Robert Levine, reflected on Mary's life and work: "Just because you have a smile on your face doesn't mean you're not ready to go to battle."

Funeral directors like those I spoke with understood how humor lightens the load and helps us through the hardest times.

Wordplay humor helps you link, lift, and lead by flipping phrases or finding the humor in life's tough moments. A playful twist can make your words unforgettable—so give them a spin!

Now it's time for another quiz:

 ## Is **Wordplay** Your Go-To Humor Tactic?

Do these statements fit your style of fun?

- ❑ I enjoy puns that make people groan *and* laugh.
- ❑ "Dad jokes" are like my second language.
- ❑ I make people laugh with the things I *say*.
- ❑ A book of funny quotations? Yes, I want to read it.
- ❑ I have a knack for funny comebacks.
- ❑ People tell me: "You're so clever!"
- ❑ "It's fourth down, and I'm punning!" describes me well.
- ❑ I like jokes that take a moment to "get," but are worth the wait.
- ❑ I love the written word! Even my emails make people smile.
- ❑ I deserve to be *pun*-ished for loving this chapter.

If you checked seven or more of these boxes, wordplay is your thing!

Clever language sparks the laughter factor faster than you can say, *"Not now, I'm going through a phrase."* This tactic is your tool for crafting zingers, puns, quips, and funny quotations that turn ordinary communication into tasty laughs. Wow them with your wit.

Wordplay—some sentences sound sensational!

## Humor Homework

Link: Is there a "word nerd" on your team who loves clever quips? Drop them a well-timed pun or dad joke. Make them your official "pun pal."

Lift: Can you reframe a dull team task with playful language? How can you turn what sounds mundane into a morale booster? Maybe rename a budget planning session a meeting of "gold diggers" to spark fun and fresh energy.

Lead: Turn a tagline into a funny brainstorm. Take one of your organizations catchphrases, like "There's no 'I' in 'team,'" or "Teamwork makes the dream work." Then invite your group to add a funny twist. *Teamwork makes the dream work—unless the dream is unlimited paid time off,* or *There's no "I" in "team," but there are two in "idiot."* How can you incorporate an exercise like this to spark a meaningful conversation about your company's values?

# TACTIC 5

# AMPLIFY

### EXAGGERATE STORIES AND SITUATIONS FOR IMPACT.

It's New Year's Day in sunny San Diego, California. A man is lounging on his couch, nursing a hangover. Suddenly, there's a knock at the door. Feeling annoyed, he opens the door.

Only to find . . . nothing.

Except, right there on his front porch is a snail.

Upset, he kicks the snail off the porch and sends it flying into the front yard.

Almost a year later, it's the day after Thanksgiving. The man, now in a food coma from eating too much turkey and stuffing, hears that familiar knock at the door.

He opens the door to see who's there. And back on the porch is the same snail!

The snail looks up and says, "What the heck was that all about?"

People get a big kick out of exaggerated stories, giant jokes, and ridiculous rants. Even if the characters are small, the laughs turn big when you use the humor tactic I call "amplify."

Are you willing to go to great lengths to get big laughs? It's easy, and it's worth it.

Amplifying is one of my favorite humor techniques. To be honest, I used to detest "over-exaggerators." (All ten trillion of them.) But, having spent decades now experiencing what makes people laugh, I stand in awe of this huge humor tactic.

Here's why this humor device devastates and delights us: *Our brains think in pictures.* When you paint big, crazy, outrageous images in people's minds, they crack up. They can't help it.

There are many ways to maximize the things you say and do to get mega-laughs. In this chapter, we plug into the power of being an exaggerator—but we will call it "amplifying." Hey, there's no reason to feel like a Big. Fat. Fibber.

## That's a Stretch

Let's start with the telling of tall tales. We love them! In her book *Wired for Story,* UCLA professor and Showtime story consultant Lisa Cron explains how our brains are neurowired for narratives.

Cron reveals that stories allow us to simulate intense experiences and relish them in a safe environment. Humans swim in stories. Larger-than-life tales have a magical effect on us.

Don't believe me? Well, believe this billionaire storyteller:

> There's always room for a story that can transport people to another place.
>
> —*J. K. Rowling*

Let's dive into what happens when we s t r e t c h jokes and stories to make them more funtastic.

Do you have a friend who can make you laugh your head off just by describing her trip to the grocery store? Chances are she actually had a fairly typical experience at the checkout line, but with the power of amplifying, she has turned a few hassles into a hilarious saga.

*Wanna be great? Exaggerate!*

When most people try to use chopsticks at a restaurant and fail, they might say, "Sheesh, I'm terrible at using chopsticks." But from the mind of an entertaining amplifier like comic-magician Steve Turner, we get this:

> The other night I ate spaghetti with chopsticks. I'm still hungry, but I knitted two pairs of socks!

This creates a crazy-funny picture in our minds. Now, notice how the following over-the-top joke does the same thing. Can you picture it in your mind? Can you hear it?

> A guy sees a sign in front of a house: "Talking Dog for Sale." He rings the bell, and the owner says, "Come on in. The dog is in the back-yard." The guy goes out and sees a nice-looking dog lounging by the pool.
>
> "So, what's your story?" he asks the dog.
>
> The dog replies, "I discovered I could talk when I was young. I joined the CIA and traveled the world as an undercover agent for eight years. When I returned to the United States I starred in several Marvel mov-ies. Recently I became an entrepreneur in the tech and aerospace industry. But now, I just live a simple life."
>
> The guy is amazed and asks the owner how much he wants for the dog.
>
> The owner says, "Fifty dollars."

"Fifty bucks? Why so cheap? It's a talking dog!"

The owner says, "Because he's a liar. He never did any of that!"

You will get big laughs when you make your jokes, stories, and personal situations *way* more outrageous.

Now let's take a deeper look at *how* you can make your laughs larger than life.

## Dramatize Details

You can make yourself the larger-than-life character in a story where you are the star. And like they say on all those dramatic shows (before the lawsuits start flying), it's "based on a true story."

Here's an example. You want to explain to your coworkers why you were late to the staff meeting. You could simply say, "Hey everybody, sorry I'm late." Or you could say something like the tall tale Julia offered to her teammates:

Sorry I'm late. (*Yawn!*) Here's how my morning went.

I woke up at 5 a.m. when my toddler greeted me screaming at the top of his lungs. Then my baby joined in with the whining.

And by "baby" I mean my husband, Tony. I stumbled out of bed barefoot, stepped on a LEGO™ car, and yelled so loud I woke up the neighbors.

They live eight houses down.

I had fifteen minutes to get ready and get my son dressed. I tripped over Tony's open laptop and smacked my head on the dresser. I made it to the bathroom, and our broken shower head fell on my head.

Breakfast was a disaster, thanks to the burned oatmeal incident. My baby didn't help. And by baby, again I mean Tony. He was asking me, "Honey, do I have clean socks somewhere?"

Outside, my car refused to start, so I grabbed my next-door neighbor's pogo stick. I started pogoing but landed in a giant pit of wet cement on our sidewalk. I finally got the car started and threw the pogo stick in the trunk. I could still hear my baby wailing, "I still can't find my socks!" Then as I drove off, I noticed I was out of gas.

It took me ten minutes to pogo to the gas station. Once I'd bounced back to the car with a well-shaken gallon of gas, I tanked up and rushed to the office.

As I pulled up, my baby texted me: "Don't worry, hon. I found the socks. I was wearing them when I went to sleep."

So, anyway . . . that's why I'm late. Any donuts left?

## Get Amped

Here are five ways to amp up the details of your story:

1. *Be super specific.* Notice how in Julia's story, she helps us imagine the experience of pogoing through cement.
2. *Add more drama.* To heighten the humor of your story, crank up the chaos.
3. *Relive your story* (don't just tell it). Let your emotions and movements increase the intensity of the tale. Make your listeners feel like it's happening right before their eyes and ears.
4. *Repeat certain elements* of your story. Julia kept referring back to her "baby" Tony. This becomes funnier when you do it three times. This is the callback technique we explored earlier. It works—but only every time!

5. *Tie the end of your story back to the beginning.* Julia sets up her rant to explain why she was late to work. She caps it again with her ending: "So, anyway . . . that's why I'm late."

Of course, you don't need to tell a looooong story to enjoy the amplifying effect. You can stress one dramatic detail, like this: My email inbox is so full, I got nominated for an episode of *Hoarders*.

## What Is "Faction"?

Amplifying your humor means more than tossing out jokes or hitting the punch line. It may require *faction*—blending fact with fiction to make your stories larger than life, and way funnier. With faction, you take everyday situations and blow them up like a balloon at a kid's birthday party—you overinflate the fact and make it "pop!"

Start with something real. Take a historical example: George Washington might not have actually chopped down that cherry tree, but the story sticks because it's rooted in truth—he was known for his honesty. We remember it not because it's a history lesson, but because it got turned into a fable.

You don't have to be a professional writer to wield faction like a samurai sword. It's a wonderful weapon for anyone who wants to generate bigger laughs by mixing fact with funny.

Begin with something real, then pump it up until it goes off the charts. Like that time you were stuck in traffic. Sure, you were bored stiff, but let's dial it up:

I was stuck in traffic for so long, I started my own podcast.

What about that new diet you're on?

I keep hunting for food I can actually eat. My husband just put a sign on the fridge that says, "We Never Close." So I tried some of those over-the-counter anti-appetite pills. I was so hungry, I ate thirty of them. Those things actually taste pretty good!

Here are some other examples:

Fact: It's hard to find a parking space at the mall.
Faction: *I circled the parking lot so many times, I'm now a mall tour guide.*

Fact: You started a new fitness routine.
Faction: *After two pushups, my fitness tracker asked, "Are you OK?"*

Fact: You work remotely.
Faction: *I've worn my sweatpants for so long, they applied for overtime.*

The secret ingredient powering faction is that it's anchored in reality. People connect with the truth in your story, but it's the wild exaggeration that gets you the laugh. "Our neighborhood is so tough, the squirrels have gang tattoos."

Creating funny faction is easy. Start with what actually happened, then let your imagination off its leash. It's like a creative workout—stretch your truth until it beefs up to six-pack abs. Better yet, eighteen-pack abs.

Maybe you didn't really get lost in the supermarket, but saying, "I spent so long wandering the aisles, I'm now the mayor of Produce" is pretty funny!

Take the truth and launch it into orbit. Make your stories big and bold, then pour on an extra splash of nonsense. And feel free to make stories up.

Remember this one? (Or did you grow up in some other galaxy?)

# Rudolph

Let's look at a classic over-the-top story.

What makes Rudolph the Red-Nosed Reindeer so inspiring? The story is not just about him—it's about you and me.

Imagine you are giving a talk about turning your "weakness" into a winning strategy. Your "weakness" may be your secret weapon.

Rudolph's nose? Total liability. Until the fog rolled in. Then suddenly Santa's like, "Hey, I've always believed in you!"

The lesson: Outsiders can step up and change everything. Rudolph wasn't exactly a regular at the reindeer games. Sometimes, it's the ones on the sidelines who can see the clearest path forward.

Also, bad weather creates great leaders! When the storm hit, Rudolph could've said, "The tribe has spoken. I'm out." Instead, he lit the way for the team.

What's *your* red nose?

What makes you different—the quirk, the challenge, the part of you that doesn't "fit"? Amplify it.

That might be your gift to share!

## So Funny

Does something make you mad? Your frustrations are funny to others when you *amplify your aggravations.*

> I went out to eat with my husband the other night. It was so loud with screaming children. We have decided to open a restaurant called "Peace and Quiet." Kids' meals start at $150.

The best humor comes from the truth—especially when you blow your pain way out of proportion. Carrie Fisher (Princess Leia in *Star Wars*) was hysterically funny in real life. She was a terrific storyteller. And what was her go-to technique? She played a game that she called "Can you *bottom this*?"

*The more you lean into your pain, and exaggerate it, the more impactful your jokes and stories become.*

Here's a humorous way you can play that game. Use the word "so" as your setup. The goal is start with something legitimately bothersome and then magnify the misery of it.

I don't know where you live. But I bet there is something frustrating about it.

Maybe you live in a cold climate like Minnesota's. It's a great state, but the weather has been described as "four months of winter and eight months of bad sledding." You might riff on this on a Zoom call, using the "so" setup.

It's *so* cold here . . .

▼ I saw a lawyer with his hands in his own pockets.
▼ My coworker spilled coffee on me, and I thanked her!
▼ I had to open the fridge to heat the house.

Now you are rocking and your team is rolling. So keep going:

I'm telling you, it's *so* cold here . . .

▼ I chipped a tooth on my soup.
▼ Our Starbucks is serving coffee on a stick.
▼ I saw a snowman knocking on people's doors, asking, "Can I come in?"

The word "so" allows you to amplify the pain and the punch line. And you can use it for just about any topic that is bugging you.

Here are other examples of how you could use "so" as a springboard:

▼ Our sales numbers were *so* low . . . we took down the monthly goal board and installed a limbo bar.
▼ The coffee at our office is *so* strong . . . we don't have creamers—we have spotters.
▼ My to-do list *so* long . . . I write it out on a CVS receipt.

# I Feel Your Pain

Hurt is what underlies most of our humor. Don't believe for a second that most comedians are always happy. Many of us are "wounded healers." This story captures the truth.

> A man goes in to see a psychiatrist, hoping to get a prescription. He's miserable. He's depressed.
>
> The doctor asks him to sit down. "What's the problem, and how can I help?"
>
> The patient responds: "I can't go on living like this. I'm so down. Life just seems pointless and sad."
>
> The doctor thinks for a moment and has an epiphany. "I know! Laughter is just what this doctor is ordering for you. Guess what? There's a circus in town starring Hillario. He's the world's funniest clown. He'll make you forget all your troubles, and you'll feel so much better."
>
> The man stares at the therapist and says, "I am Hillario."

This story isn't just another punch line—it's a glimpse into how humor often comes from a place of pain. Comedy can turn our struggles into something powerful. The idea of the wounded healer rings true for all of us because it's through our own challenges that we find the humor to share.

Some of the funniest material comes from the darkest places. The sadness, frustration, and challenges we face become fuel for humor. It's about not hiding our pain but amplifying it to make the laughter (and links) even stronger!

The more you lean into your pain, and exaggerate it, the more impactful your jokes and stories become.

As humor beings, we are all wounded healers. You can link with your listeners when you open up about your struggles. It's through your own difficulties that you will discover the maximum mirth.

Some good news: Humor doesn't just make the pain bearable; it can give you—and those around you—power over it. When we amplify our pain, we increase the impact of our jokes and stories while simultaneously feeling better.

Think about it. How many times have you shared a story that was painful at the time, only to have it become a go-to joke later? By embracing the tough stuff, we find the biggest laughs.

And that, my friend, is the true healing power of comedy. Laugh it *up*.

## Let's Go Crazy

When your humor tactic is to amplify your stories, you plug into the electrifying power of *exaggeration*.

---

### HUMOR HERO: Mike Lukas

Mike Lukas, a husband and father of two in Dallas, Texas, is a busy freelance writer producing a thousand words daily. He is the author of *My Daily Joy Strategy*. As a humor coach, Mike helps people discover their "comedy lens"—a unique comedic perspective on life. He teaches how to amplify everyday absurdities for bigger laughs, explaining, "You'll get more laughs at work and in relationships by exaggerating what aggravates you."

**Tips from Mike for amplifying laughter and happiness:**

▼ Heighten your humor. Don't just say, "My son is on his phone too much." Try this: "Verizon gave my son his own cell tower."

▼ Want to be happier? Identify your joy buttons and focus on them daily.

▼ Find your funny muscle and flex it. Like any muscle, it strengthens with use!

---

Take a story or a situation and inflate it to cartoonish proportions. It's the art of turning a molehill into a mountain—and then snowboarding down with a big smile on your face.

Put your story on steroids! This tactic isn't about playing it safe. It's about stretching the truth until it snaps—and they smile:

▼ I know I am overweight. The census has me listed in two zip codes!

▼ I drink a lot of coffee. My Starbucks just installed a second drive-thru lane for me.

▼ I'm not saying my dog is more popular than yours—but does your pet have a social media manager?

When professional comedians describe how they impact an audience, they amplify it. They say, "I killed." "I destroyed." "They were busting a gut!" Of course, when it doesn't go so well, they exaggerate too: "I bombed!"

Using this humor tool means you skip the subtlety and crank everything up louder, making it wilder and more outrageous. The further you go, the funnier it gets.

You are not turning the volume up a bit. You are going to "11." Acoustic guitar? No. You go metal. As Ozzy Osbourne would say, "I'm going off the rails on a crazy train."

## Making *Big* Impressions

Going *big* gets big laughs. It's one thing to hear a story told straight; it's another thing to hear an embellished version. Extremes are a good thing in humor—so if you can overstate it, you're doing it right.

Extremes work in two directions, of course. *Understatement* can also amplify the funny. Check out the ending to this classic joke:

Two Texans are sitting on a plane. An old man has the seat between them.

The first Texan says, "I own thirty thousand acres with a thousand head of cattle. They call my place the Ropin' Ranch."

The second Texan says, "I own three hundred thousand acres with ten thousand head of cattle. We call my place the Big Ranch."

They look at the old man, who says, "I own only three hundred acres."

The first Texan laughs and asks, "Three hundred acres? What do you call it?"

The rich old man says, "Downtown Dallas."

## Kiddin' Around

Going small can also be very funny. Tremendous laughs often come from tiny humans. Kids say outrageous things.

When my youngest son James was just five, my dad, who was seventy-five, took him out for breakfast.

My dad told James, "I'm your grandpa, and I'm taking you to breakfast. Maybe one day when you are older, you will take your grandson out for breakfast." James said, "Yeah. But you'll be dead."

The all-time legends of laughter, like Robin Williams, imitated kids. If you feel embarrassed acting like a child, you can still get big laughs by simply repeating things they say!

I'm going to marry Mom when I grow up because she already knows how to make spaghetti and I don't want to teach anyone else.

—*Ethan, seven*

When I grow up, I'm going to be a superhero. My superpower will be eating all the candy.

—*Chloe, six*

Why don't grown-ups get stickers when they do a good job?

—*Mia, six*

I cleaned my room, but the toys decided to come out and play again!

—*Dylan, five*

There is more we can learn from kids, when it comes to turning up the fun.

## Ham It Up

To bring your humor to life, become larger than life. Ham it up! Expand your ability to entertain with bold expressions, movements, and more.

### Big Faces

Making funny faces is a gift to others. Roll your eyes, raise your eyebrows, or pretend to cry—your face is a projector screen. Exaggerated expressions often get bigger laughs than the joke itself. Sometimes, though, a straight-faced deadpan is the funniest move of all.

### Big Moves

Physical comedy speaks volumes. From Will Smith's antics on *The Fresh Prince* to Daniel LaBelle's YouTube genius, bold movements amplify laughs. LaBelle has about forty million subscribers. When you think your moves feel like too much, that probably means you are just getting started.

### Big Characters

Do you have a larger-than-life relative who steals the show at family gatherings? Channel them! Big, outrageous characters stick in people's minds.

At Thanksgiving one year, my eight-year-old cousin was wearing a sweater with a picture of a dog on it. So, did I bark like a dog every time I saw her that night? Heck no. That's what an amateur would do. I barked, panted, wagged my tail, raised my leg, put my plate on the floor, and ate from it like a dog's bowl. For two minutes. *Every* time I saw her that night.

Because I'm a professional.

Anyone can do an impression of Daffy Duck on the way to the car in the Disneyland parking lot. Only a pro like Ken Newman will keep doing that impression the entire ride home. All forty-five minutes. All while telling outrageous jokes.

He's a professional.

### Big Accessories

Forget clown costumes. A funny hat or oversized jacket can deliver large laughs before you even speak. Props aren't just gags; they transform the way you feel, move, and interact. When you ham it up, bigger really is better. So go big—your audience will thank you.

But even more important than what you wear is how you show up.

# Get Real

When you see a fantastic comedian, one who has you "rolling on the floor," you tell your friends, "It was like he knew exactly what I have to deal with!" The comic is magnifying your feelings, your experience, and your pain. He is just doing it to the *max*.

Amplifying your humor plays big to an entire group. But even as you pump up punch lines, keep this in mind: You want to connect your pain and your punch lines with what's real for you. That begins when you are honest (in a heightened and humorous way) about your own feelings.

Heartfelt humor comes from genuine feelings.

In the movie *Her*, Joaquin Phoenix's character, Theodore, falls for an AI character named Samantha (voiced by Scarlett Johansson). He thinks she's the one—until he asks if she's chatting with anyone else. Turns out Samantha is connecting with 8,316 humans. Oh, and she's in love with 641 of them! Ouch. Don't be "her."

Be big. But be you.

Whether you're speaking to a tiny group or a large crowd, or delivering your TED talk to the whole world, approach it like you're having a personal chat with a friend.

## Go for a Three-Peat

Good things come in threes, and so do great jokes. Why? Because three is the magic number that keeps your audience hooked . . . and then hits them hard!

A joke builds to a funny finale when you let it unfold in a three-part sequence. It's the secret to amplifying your material, growing it right into the punch line.

The rule of threes is simple. Three is the smallest number that lets you make a pattern and then break that pattern. The first item sets the stage, the second builds anticipation, and the third delivers a knockout punch. It's a structure that maximizes rhythm and impact in your humor, making each laugh linger longer.

Friends, Romans, debt collectors . . .

For lunch we're featuring liverwurst, fried clams, and Pepto-Bismol.

My daughter wants to be a lawyer. My son wants to be a musician. And my wife wants to be single.

The power of three is sensational. But it's more than a trick—it's a fundamental way our brains process information. It's why stories, speeches, and jokes that use this structure stick with us long after we've heard them. Whether you're trying to get a laugh or make a point, using a three-part sequence helps your message land with greater impact.

> You can't fly anywhere these days. I had breakfast in Orlando, lunch in Dallas, and my luggage is in Milwaukee.

Even in life's everyday moments, the power of three shines through:

**DAD:** Son, you better wake up.
**SON:** I don't want to go to school.
**DAD:** Why not?
**SON:** Here are three reasons: It's boring. I hate it. The kids make fun of me.
**DAD:** I'll give you three reasons why you have to go.
　　You are supposed to be there.
　　You are forty-five years old.
　　You're the principal!

Remember, the best things come in threes. I just confirmed this with me, myself, and I.

Next time you're crafting (or looking for) a joke, consider making it a three-peat. It's a quick, effective way to amplify your humor—and keep your audience listening . . . and laughing.

## Is This Thing On?

Let's talk about amplification—literally. Bringing the laughter factor into any setting starts with people actually hearing you. It's not just about speaking louder. Make sure your voice carries, whether in a small room or a packed crowd.

Take it from me: Even the best joke tanks if no one hears the punch line.

I once emceed an event at a fancy Napa Valley hotel where rooms cost over $1,000 a night, and iced tea set you back $12. Yet somehow, they didn't have an outdoor sound system—no mics, no speakers, just me and my voice competing with cocktail chatter.

With minutes to spare, I had to corral people from the courtyard to the ballroom. Shouting wasn't an option. Instead, I grabbed a spoon and an empty wine glass from a server. *Ding, ding, ding!* The gentle chime cut through the buzz, and all eyes turned to me. "Friends, it's time to head inside," I announced. No yelling, no drama—just a simple trick to command attention.

If you want people to laugh at your jokes, they need to hear you first. *Ding, ding, ding!* Here are a few sound tips to help you "ring" true:

▼ *Make sure you're mic ready.* My go-to is a wireless handheld mic. It makes you sound better, lets you move freely, and spares you the hassle of untangling an over-the-ear mic from your hat or hair.

▼ *Stand up.* Standing gives you authority and helps your voice carry farther—just like a teacher commanding a classroom.

▼ *Project your voice.* Speak clearly and with energy. You don't need to yell, but don't mumble, either—confidence in your tone makes all the difference.

Speaking of clear communication, here's one I heard at a senior center:

Two older men are chatting. The first says, "Hey, Ron, I got a new hearing aid!"

Ron replies, "That's great! What kind is it?"

The first guy answers, "About 4:30."

You don't want your message to get lost like that. Whether it's a heartfelt story or a punch line, make sure your audience hears you loud and clear.

Next time you step up to speak, ask yourself: *Is this thing on?* Raise your voice, and you'll raise your impact.

## Paint with Numbers

When I was a kid, McDonald's restaurants used to proudly post the specific number of hamburgers they had sold on a giant sign below their golden arches. My sister and I loved to see how the digits climbed higher and higher every month. This reminds me of a joke:

> My friend ate at McDonald's so often, he'd sit in the parking lot just to watch the sign change!

Eventually, McDonald's had sold such a quantity of hamburgers that the company apparently lost track of the specific number. It switched to a vague "Millions and Millions Served." Finally, that sign came down, and the prices went up. Recently, I bought a Happy Meal, and I was . . . until I got to the payment window.

*When you want to amplify your humor, sometimes it's a numbers game.*

Statistics make us want to hit the snooze button. But when you jack those numbers up and weave them into your jokes and stories, suddenly stats become something else—something funny.

We've talked about the power of three-peats in humor. Now, let's look at how numbers create big reactions when you exaggerate them.

There's a reason funny little stories feel way bigger when you play by the numbers.

I took a pole and found out 100 percent of people were mad when the tent collapsed.

My Uncle Joe used to say, "You can eat any dessert you want, as long as you eat only three bites." (Joe weighed 325 pounds. Those were big bites.)

I went to a buffet and ate 7,000 calories. The dessert was so rich, it came with its own financial advisor!

Numbers don't have to be big to get big laughs. Sometimes the humor comes from making them small—or just absurd. Scott Wood, one of the funniest comedians I know, once said, "We had a small wedding. Fifty to seventy-five . . . dollars."

Numbers give your humor something special: specificity. And padding those numbers makes them vivid in our minds.

You can turn a typical statement into something terrific. Our parents didn't usually lecture us by saying, "I've told you time and again." No, they went big: "I've told you this a million times . . ."

In humor, numbers transform arithmetic into amusement. They're weapons that expand your wit. Next time you're crafting a joke, remember: The number doesn't have to be accurate; it needs to be outlandish—and specific.

Whether you're referring to a 12-cent tip or a 30,000-calorie snack that comes with a 37-year gym membership, usually the bigger the number, the bigger the laugh.

Paint with numbers, and you can count on more laughs.

What's the bottom line? Go *big* with your jokes, details, visuals, expressions, and numbers. You'll be doing more than telling a funny joke or sharing a humorous story—you'll leave a lasting mark. Your goal is to *amplify* the effect on your audience.

This strategy lifts you and everybody *up*.

Exaggerate your rants, your remarks, and your routines. You will make the experience feel bigger . . . and better.

More good news: Gut-busting humor counts as cardio.

Ready for another quiz?

## ✓ Is **Amplify** Your Go-To Humor Tactic?

Are these statements true of you?

❑ I can turn a simple story into an epic tale.

❑ I love exaggerating everyday situations for maximum comedic effect.

❑ My "traffic was terrible" story could win me an Oscar.

❑ I'm the person who says, "And then it got even crazier!"

❑ I turn family vacations into "you won't believe what happened" sagas.

❑ I add dramatic sound effects to make a story even funnier.

❑ I laugh hardest when the absurdity of a situation is dialed up to 11.

❑ For me, "too much" is just the right amount of funny.

❑ If something is worth laughing at, it's worth stretching it into a story.

❑ I think this book should cost *more*.

If you checked seven or more of these boxes, you are ready for the "big time."

Heighten the humor in your stories and jokes—turn the ordinary into the extraordinary. Exaggerate (more than anyone in the galaxy)! Don't hold back. Turn frustrations into fun. Stretch your stories into outrageous tall tales, then watch how the laughter grows.

Amplify your humor. Life is too short for little laughs.

# Humor Homework

Link: How can you playfully amplify a shared interest or location when connecting with a potential customer? Example: "You graduated from Notre Dame? I'm jealous. I love the Fighting Irish. I've seen the movie *Rudy* fifteen times!"

Lift: What funny frustration can you stretch to comic extremes? How can you exaggerate a teammate's success in a way that also honors them? Create an over-the-top compliment for a teammate: "Your idea was so electric, Nikola Tesla just followed you on LinkedIn!"

Lead: How can you amplify the humor in your leadership style? Think *big*. Tell a tall tale. Make your details larger than life. Add a visual that gets a huge laugh. Could an unexpected prop turn your message into a showstopper? Nobody forgets a meeting that opens with a CEO riding in on a unicycle!

# LEADING WITH
# LAUGHTER

## LET HUMOR **OPEN** DOORS AND HEARTS IN YOUR ORGANIZATION.

### The Management Test

A CEO is interviewing three candidates for a key management role. She asks each one the same question: "What is two plus two?"

The first candidate is an engineer. He pulls out a calculator, punches the numbers, and answers, "Four."

The second candidate is a sales executive. She says, "Well, the engineers will tell you 'four,' but I can get it to you for three-and-a-half. Three-point-two in bulk."

The final candidate is an accountant. He leans in and whispers, "What do you want it to be?"

# Find Your Funny

As a leader, the first words out of your mouth—along with your attitude—reveal who you are.

You must decide: *Do I want to harness my sense of humor?*

Once you commit, immediately begin to engage with your go-to humor style. Figure out which humor tactics suit you best and use them. What's *your* laugh language?

*The Laughter Factor* has equipped you with tools to create more fun. But don't spoil the party. Avoid these three "P" topics in your company or group:

- ▼ No politics
- ▼ No prejudice
- ▼ No profanity

Not sure whether you're crossing a line? My motto again: If in doubt, leave it out.

This chapter is meant for you if you are—or want to become—a leader. It's for readers who lead groups of any size. We'll talk about how the laughter factor helps you connect, empower, and guide people.

Let's reinforce and dig deeper here into the impact you can have when you link, lift, and lead with humor.

*Laughter unlocks leadership.*

In case you missed the memo, let me remind you. Humor helps—big-time. Laughter

- ▼ releases endorphins, instantly lifting spirits
- ▼ builds community, making teams more cohesive
- ▼ reduces stress and de-escalates drama
- ▼ sparks creativity and fresh perspectives

And yes, it even boosts productivity. (Funny really *is* money!)

Maybe adding the laughter factor to your group won't save you from an audit, but it *will* make you the kind of leader people actually want to follow. Bring the laughter—it's the only leadership tool that doesn't require a budget line, an MBA, or a three-hour meeting to implement.

By bringing the laughter factor to your group, you empower everybody to feel better. *Together.* Like the coach in the following story did.

## Don't Give Up. *Laugh It* Up.

At halftime, the coach could see that his basketball team was on the verge of quitting. He called for their attention and declared:

"The great ones are *remembered* for not giving up!"

Some players rolled their eyes. Others looked down.

"Did Michael Jordan give up?"

The players said quietly, "No."

He continued, "Did Larry Bird, Steph Curry, or Caitlin Clark give up?"

They responded more emphatically, "No!"

"Did Ernest Peabody give up?"

There was a big silence. One player said, "Who? We've never heard of him."

The coach said, "Exactly. Because he gave up!"

When it comes to leading with laughter, you just need to get started. Humor will make you more memorable as a speaker, manager, and influencer.

Of course, it comes with a catch. You must commit to it. As a leader, it starts with you.

## The Show before the Show . . .

Here's a secret to great presentations.

There's always a show *before* the show.

Whatever stage you're stepping onto—a meeting, a presentation, or that first dinner with the in-laws—your performance equals your preparation.

I once saw a super-famous speaker flop. He'd assumed his reputation was enough. "Hey, everyone, I'm here." His audience saw through it. He wasn't ready for them. He didn't connect.

Being there isn't enough. Be there *before* you get there.

Even the greats don't "wing it"—they prepare to fly.

---

## LINK

## Discover Your Team's Laugh Languages

You now have the tactics for being funny. But don't just make 'em laugh. Here's another vital strategy to take to heart:

*Laugh at other people's jokes and stories.*

Get to know and enjoy *their* humor tactics. Remember, your teammates, clients, and students are absorbed in a never-ending struggle to think well of themselves. When *you* laugh at their humor, they feel better about who they are.

As self-absorbed humans, we are naturally tempted to listen to others just long enough so we can chime in with our own story or joke. Resist that impulse! Listen. Don't just wait until you can respond. Listen. Enjoy your teammates when they tap into their types of humor. You will make them feel important. And *this* is perhaps the most important job of any leader: valuing and validating your people.

## What Mistakes Can I Avoid When I Am Coordinating an Event?

Planning an event is a lot like juggling—except the balls are on fire, and your people are watching!

The following pitfalls can trip up *any* event involving people, plans, and communication. Avoid them, and your audience will be saying "Wow!" instead of "Whoa."

▼ *Seating the audience too far away.* Ever tried connecting with someone who feels like they're in another zip code? Keep your audience close enough to feel the energy. (But not so close they can share the speaker's water bottle).

▼ *Forgetting the fun.* People come for the content but stay for the connections. A little laughter or surprise goes a long way. Pro tip: Laughter is the universal language of engagement.

▼ *Not hiring a pro emcee.* Think one of your staff can fill in as the host? Think again. An experienced emcee can engage and entertain your audience!

▼ *Forgetting to brief presenters.* Winging it isn't just bad for emcees—it's a recipe for disaster with speakers, too. A one-page run-of-show document avoids those "Oh, I thought I was going on after lunch!" moments.

▼ *Skipping a pre-event "huddle."* The "pow" happens in the planning. A ten-minute huddle with the AV team and presenters ensures that everyone knows their role. This way, no one springs on you, "Hey, I need a podium."

I know an experienced sales leader named Tom Sweeny who introduced a colleague to me like this: "This is Rebecca. She is a gifted chef and a creative wizard." She lit up like a Christmas tree. Then he leaned over and whispered to me:

*"People want to feel discovered."*

Tom models this method. He is a curator of connections and knows how to make people feel good about themselves. Instead of trying to show how talented he is, he celebrates the talents of those around him. You can, too.

Lead your team, staff, employees, and audience into the wonderful experience of shared delight. It pays to amuse and to be amused.

*A culture of fun is good for everyone.*

## Don't Get Smart with Me

Too many leaders think they need to constantly present themselves as intellectuals or experts. Don't fall into that trap.

Want to see how lonely that path can be? Do a Google image search and look at the portraits of the twenty-eight greatest philosophers, according to Oxford University Press. They're some of the saddest, loneliest faces you'll ever see!

You might be an introvert. That's OK. But don't be an isolator.

Brainiac loners rarely make great leaders. Your team doesn't need you to prove your brilliance. They'll be drawn to your warmth, wit, and wisdom—in that order.

The shortest course on human relations is found in just two words in E. M. Forster's *Howards End*:

Only connect.

Humor allows you to do just that, and it's way more fun than writing the 337th Amazon book on stoicism.

Dr. Patch Adams said, "Happiness is the most radical act." And he was right—especially when it comes to bonding with your team. Being a leader is like being a doctor—but don't try explaining *that* to HR.

Patch knew that humor is vital for healing—not just for patients but also for those who care for them. In a world filled with stress and exhaustion, laughter rejuvenates our hearts.

As a leader, you never want to act childish; however, embracing a "childlike" sense of humor helps your team to avoid burnout. Enjoy yourself. A good laugh is like pressing Ctrl+Alt+Del on your group's stress levels.

Laughter lightens your load, boosts your mood, and spreads joy like free donuts. And put this sticky note on your mirror:

Humor isn't just for them—it's for me, too.

## Crowd Work

As an interactive speaker and host, I love to engage in what comedians call "crowd work."

But here's the thing: I never see an audience as a "crowd." To me, every audience member is a friend.

There are three things I've discovered about building community quickly—whether you're leading, speaking, hosting, or presenting:

### Proximity

Get close to people. Step off the platform. Connection happens when you're physically near them.

### Participation

Involve them. People can't be bored when you make them part of the action! Yes, being funny helps. But again, you don't have to be a stand-up. Just help everyone have *fun*.

## Personalization

Greet people by name. Remember their faces. Make it conversational. A common mistake I see newbie speakers make is that they focus so much on content, content, content—but what we're really after is connection.

And since you've read this far . . . here's an extra key for you:

## Purpose

Remember the mission of your meeting. Invite people into that purpose—it's what unites everyone.

How might you connect with your "crowd" to build community? Here's an easy way.

## Icebreakers

In the past three decades of my career inspiring laughter and life change, I have learned the power of warming up a group.

Whether you are hosting an event, stepping up as a guest speaker, or serving as the master of ceremonies, a great icebreaker can transform the energy in a room (even a Zoom room).

Here are three tips for awesome icebreakers:

1. *Make it fun.* Start with something that gets a laugh or a smile—humor is the fastest way to warm people up.
2. *Make it interactive.* Get everyone involved. Icebreakers aren't about information; they're about engagement. Ask a fun question like, "What's the one movie you've watched more than any other flick?"
3. *Make it about them.* Focus on your listeners. Skip stories about yourself; ask questions and create moments that highlight *their* experiences. Invite people to share.

A good icebreaker isn't about the content you share—it's about connecting with your audience. You want to set a warm and relational tone for your meeting, and celebrate your people! Here's how:

▼ *Break the tension.* A well-timed joke or icebreaker can turn awkward silence into social glue. ("Hey, we have challenges . . . but we also have snacks.")
▼ *Encourage real talk.* Ask for feedback and listen—without sending anyone to "timeout."
▼ *Share the spotlight.* Hear and highlight your team's ideas and let them take charge.

Why does it matter? One study from Oxford University suggests workplaces that foster fun and humor see up to a 30 percent increase in productivity (and creativity!).

People who share humor feel more . . . human.

Here's how to make the shift:

▼ Stop trying to be "the boss," and use humor to connect in playful ways. Your team may work harder, and they will trust you more.
▼ Ask yourself, *Am I building a culture of connection—or fear?*
▼ Lead with laughter and watch your team thrive.

## LIFT

In a famous scene in the movie *Goodfellas*, Joe Pesci's character, Tommy DeVito, asks: "I'm funny how? I mean funny like I'm a clown? I amuse you?"

It's a terrifying moment. We imagine the worst is about to happen.

Fortunately for fellow mobster Henry Hill, played by Ray Liotta, ultimately the tension breaks, and the *amusement* lifts the energy of the room.

Speaking of a-muse-ing . . .

In Greek mythology, Thalia was the muse of comedy. She brought laughter and joy wherever she went. She inspired unity, creativity, and camaraderie. Thalia is often depicted in art with a comedy mask, a shepherd's staff, and a big smile. Her name fittingly means "to flourish." If you want to have an impact on people, your name should stand for "flourish," too. (Even if your name is currently "Amanda.")

## Don't Speak *at*, Speak *into*

As a leader, you can maximize the uplift factor. Here are five ways you can speak *into* a program:

1. *Maximize the run of show (agenda).* Collaborate with your event coordinator (or be that person, if you don't have one). Make the sequence sing. Are you creating moments that inspire?
2. *Reinforce the meeting's mission.* What's the big idea that you want to have stick? Make it so memorable that your attendees can't stop talking about it—on the way home and before next year's meeting.
3. *Shine a light on key players.* Spotlight the MVPs in the room: customers, donors, or partners. Show them they're valued; make them feel celebrated.
4. *Add energy.* Kick things off with pizzazz and pump the momentum during your talk. Close with impact. Your energy sets the tone and keeps everyone engaged.
5. *Spring surprises!* Every great event needs a little magic. Create some unexpected "Wow!" moments to keep people buzzing long after the event.

Speaking *into* an event isn't about delivering words—it's about creating lots of liftoff: moments that elevate the experience.

# Entertain to Empower

Levity lifts. You really don't have to put on a Vegas show to bring way more fun to work and relationships. The goal isn't to get a standing ovation (though if that happens, soak it up); it's really about making those around you feel at ease.

*Just lighten the mood.*

Ask yourself, "How can I bring a little laughter to this situation?" Maybe it's kicking off a staff meeting with a joke about your previous job:

*Humor will make you more memorable as a speaker, manager, and influencer.*

> "I used to sell home security systems. It was so easy. I went door to door. If the customer wasn't home, I'd just leave my brochure on their kitchen table."

It's true. Your people will like you more if you invite them to laugh.

Leaders serve. So, dish up some fun! When you help your team laugh through difficult times, you help them feel superior to challenges. Good times, experienced together, become core to a culture of staying connected.

There is a wonderful African proverb: "If you want to go fast, go alone. If you want to go far, go together."

We can spin it this way here: "If you want to feel isolated, laugh alone. If you want to feel like a team, laugh together."

Humor enhances thinking and productivity. Some of the best stories you can tell are the ones that will get your people laughing and thinking.

Imagine you're giving a talk about growing profits in your organization. You could kick it off like this:

> "I have been asked to talk about sales growth in today's economy. And I know why they asked me. *I'm a walking economy.* My hairline is in recession, and my stomach is experiencing inflation."

## HUMOR HEROES: Scott Meltzer and Katrine Spang-Hanssen

Scott Meltzer and Katrine Spang-Hanssen, better known as Scotty and Trink, are communication and event specialists. They are masters at blending humor with corporate messaging. Based in San Francisco, they travel the world, turning product presentations and sales meetings into captivating experiences. Having performed in multiple languages for many culturally diverse audiences, they've seen that humor transcends all barriers.

What's their secret to making fun functional? They say, "Collaboration! The best connections happen when people create laughter together."

**Here are Scott and Trink's tips for leading with laughter:**

▼ **Team up.** Humor thrives on collaboration. Build on each other's ideas, and the sparks (and smiles) will ignite.

▼ **Be spontaneous.** The biggest laughs come when the humor feels authentic. Prepare, but be open to the moment.

▼ **Practice!** Like any skill, humor improves when you use it often. Whether crafting punch lines or juggling funny ideas, keep at it.

## Leverage the Laughter

Before diving into a joke, a funny rant, or an icebreaker, ask yourself:

*Is this fun?*
*Is it helpful?*
*Is it right for my group?*

Humor isn't just about goofing around—though there's a time and place for that, too. At its core, humor is always one thing: fun. Even if you *still* think you aren't funny, you can always establish more fun in your group.

Don't stress too much about *how* you deliver a joke; just focus on getting people laughing. My friend Sandy Chanley, who has produced comedy specials for Chris Rock, Jeff Foxworthy, and other top comedians, often reminds me, "Funny is funny." And the laughter that follows is proof.

Consider this: Preschoolers laugh 450 times a day. Adults? Just 15. Guess who's less stressed?

Sharing a laugh with your team sends a powerful message: *We're in this together, and we'll be OK.* Although it might sound like a cliché, it's true—laughter reduces stress. That's why it's called "comic relief."

If you amuse people in appropriate ways, you'll discover that *laughter liberates.* It allows you to confront tough issues in a more digestible way.

Don't worry if you haven't perfected your brand of humor yet. Just make them smile in the ways that only you can. They'll be glad they know you. Remember the old adage from show business: "Always leave 'em laughing."

## More Windows, Less Lumber

Let's talk about weaving humor into your presentations. Great leaders don't just offer a plan—they lift hearts. Laughter lightens the load, making your message more engaging and your audience more receptive.

So, sprinkle in lighthearted jokes or personal anecdotes that connect with your audience. You want them thinking, *Hey, this is actually enjoyable!* Tell stories to illustrate your core message. As a friend of mine, the fantastic speaker Bill Butterworth, says, "Constructing a speech is like building a house. You want more windows, less lumber."

A funny story makes your points vivid and memorable. Remember: *Facts tell. Stories sell.* Even a simple anecdote can highlight your key point. Test your jokes with trusted peers, fine-tune them, and trust your gut—it's all about what resonates with your group.

And don't forget your opening and closing. Start with a joke or story that sets the tone and hooks your audience. End with a humorous story that reinforces your message and leaves them inspired.

Finally, reach their hearts. There is a story of two speakers in ancient Greece. After Demosthenes spoke, the crowd marveled: "What a brilliant mind!" But after Philip of Macedon addressed them, they shouted, "Let's march!" The lesson? Great communicators move hearts, not just minds. Don't forget: Humor helps you reach their hearts.

## LEAD

To lead people with positive humor, we have to be intentional about giving them the gift of laughter. When it comes to fun, they'll follow if you go first.

Then again, sometimes you need to receive what you give. So, remember to receive the lift of laughter yourself. Buy a book of dad jokes. Take an improv class. Watch a funny film before your next important talk. Lighten up. As G. K. Chesterton said, "Angels can fly because they take themselves lightly."

## Humor Helps

When you think about your organization, team, nonprofit, classroom, church, or business, *what do you want it to be?*

What counts most in your organization? If you believe people matter, remember that *laughing matters.* Foster more fun, and you build emotional bridges.

*To connect with people, you've got to feel what they feel.*

And we all want to feel good.

Using humor strategically is a catalyst—it kickstarts ideas, builds instant camaraderie, and helps your people finish strong. Want to break the ice? Bring in the laughter factor. Humor sparks engagement, turning strangers into newfound friends. Stuck in a rut of tedious routines? Bust out of that rut with a zany change of pace. Is your team daunted by the challenges they face? Relieve the stress with the comfort of shared laughter; they'll tackle those tough issues with renewed energy.

Hey, are you smiling yet? If not, here are some quick examples you could use with your team.

*You want to get the most out of a work session:*
"The worst thing about office parties? Looking for a new job the next day! So, let's make today something we can all be proud of."

*You aim to improve quality in your business:*
"What do you call a factory that makes good products but not great ones? A satis-factory. But we can be so much more than that."

*You're giving a talk about moving forward:*
"If the opposite of pro is con, then the opposite of progress is . . . ?" (Audience answers, "congress.") "And together, we are going to do so much better than that."

## A Comedian's Confession

I am the leader of a funny business, yet I sometimes forget to follow my own advice and let the light of laughter in. Worse, I often forget to encourage my team—yes, even in the feel-good business—to lighten up. Here's your reminder:

*Be down to clown.*

You set the tone. If you're not entertaining your people, you're not engaging them. No need for silly suits or juggling rubber chickens—just create a culture that values humor, inclusion, and well-being. As my mom used to say, "Get it? Got it? Good!" My mom is a court jester in her own right.

Lead from "Ha ha!" to "Aha!" Laughter inspires breakthroughs. Encourage humor as a habit—because humor is not just for pro laugh-makers: It's for you and your people.

Remember the famous saying: "Laughter is the best medicine"? Well, not always. The British comedian Jasper Carrott once pointed out that "laughter is the best medicine—unless you're diabetic; then insulin comes pretty high on the list."

So go ahead. Inject them with a shot of "*grin*sulin." Your group will feel better immediately.

## "I'm Still Not Sure Humor Will Work for Me"

Be of good cheer. You *can* make people laugh. Not sure where to start? You can't go wrong telling a good story. Here is a surefire formula for making your stories more entertaining.

This formula flows like a funnel. And what comes out? Laughter.

I will share the sequence. Then I will show you an example of the kind of humorous story you can create and share. Use it as an opener or icebreaker, or when you've run out of weather talk and magic tricks.

First, here's the formula:

> You start with a main character—specifically you.
> Things seem to be just fine when suddenly . . .
> You are hit by some kind of calamity.
> Next comes the crazy twist.
> The story ends.
> You pause.
> Ha!

Now let's see it in action, Imagine your name is Melanie, and you share this story:

> I signed up for a beginner yoga workshop to de-stress. But I accidentally joined the advanced class!
>
> It was packed with people stretching and meditating and otherwise yoga-ing. I was doing pretty well, until they instructed us all to do a handstand.
>
> I had it going for about three seconds, and then I toppled right over like I'd been smacked by gravity. This set off a chain reaction with the other students. Knocking each other off our mats. It was like everybody was a pin, and I was the bowling ball.
>
> I felt feet flying at me.
>
> The yoga instructor said, "Well done, Melanie! You just initiated a ritual we call 'the *wave* of relaxation.'"
>
> The other students kicked me out of the class. Literally. You'd think that, as an advanced yoga class, they'd be more chill about toppling.

If you have read the preceding chapters, you may have noticed something about Melanie's story: It features all five of our humor tactics!

▼ It feels like an *in-joke* because she let us in on her stress. And we can all relate to that.
▼ She *pokes* fun at herself because she couldn't stand on her hands.
▼ The story is *amplified* because she stretched the truth about people tumbling down all around her.

▼ *Wordplay* is happening with her bowling metaphor.

▼ And Melanie's story has a *surprise* "kicker" at the end!

## You Just Got Another Bonus

Here are (almost) ten tips to help you incorporate the laughter factor to make work more playful:

1. *Start with a smile.* Even if it feels fake, smiles are contagious—and yours will turn real soon enough.
2. *Know your crowd.* Listen first, laugh second. Tailor your humor to connect in meaningful ways.
3. *Open up.* Share your human side. Your pain can be their gain, and vulnerability inspires connection.
4. *Break the ice.* Skip the monologue and spark conversations. Icebreakers make meetings less frozen.
5. *Spot the bright side.* Be a human highlighter. "When life gives you lemons . . . build a lemonade stand!"
6. *Lead with respect.* Keep it positive and inclusive—make everyone feel like an insider.
7. *Stay tuned in.* If your humor isn't landing, adjust. The goal is simple: Make them glad.
8. *Encourage play.* Foster a playful culture. Laughter builds morale and bonds teams.
9. *Reflect and grow.* Hone your humor skills—professional laugh-makers practice, and so should you.

Why am I giving only nine tips and not ten? Like a great punch line, it's all about your reaction!

So, I invite you to create tip 10. Write down the biggest laugh lesson you have learned from this book. Add yours to make the list a solid ten. Here. I'll leave some space for you to fill in.

My Big Laugh Lesson:

_____

Humor works like rubber cement for leaders—it glues your group together. You are more persuasive when you are more playful. Feel-good humor builds trust. Weave laughter into your leadership. Your team will thank you for it.

*Lead with laughter—because your people are silently begging to have more fun.*

## Humor Homework

Link: Foster fun connections by starting a laugh-out-loud tradition. Imagine a "Throwback Thursday" lunch where employees bring a favorite childhood meal. (SpaghettiOs, Hot Pockets, Lunchables, anyone?) Cap it off by voting for the funniest lunch. Then, surprise the winner with a gift card for the best restaurant in town!

Lift: How can you encourage others with *their* favorite form of fun? Listen to your team. What tickles their funny bones—clever quips, quick jokes, or lighthearted banter? Even a thoughtful "gag gift" can show appreciation. Surprise your assistant with a personalized superhero cape and a note: "Maria, you make our sales soar!"

Lead: Harness your favorite humor tactic—surprise, poke, in-jokes, wordplay, or amplify. Choose a laugh lane and have fun with it. Start with your destination in mind. Now ask yourself: *How will I use my humor to lead people there with laughter?* Example: If wordplay is your favorite technique, write a funny poem about the CRM migration you are prepping for your team. Take a famous title and make it your own: "The Road Not Synced," "Leads of Grass," "The List That Stole Christmas."

# FOR FURTHER FUN

## Q & A: Funny You Should Ask

**Q. I'm still not sure about my laugh language. What do you recommend?**

**A.** To discover your unique sense of humor, start by asking yourself *What do I find funny?* If you enjoy inside jokes, focus on that style. If puns make you laugh, you'll likely excel at crafting and delivering language-based humor. Pay attention to things you say or do that tend to make people around you laugh. Then, do more of that!

**Q. How should I respond when they don't laugh?**

**A.** First, here's how *not* to respond: with nervous laughter of your own. When there's a beat of silence after a joke, don't fill it with your laughter. Give it an extra second or two. Breathe. Stay composed. Most of the time, the laughter will come. If it doesn't, that's OK. Move on. Avoid the mistake of blaming your listeners by saying, "Oh, you didn't get it!" This can embarrass them and you. If the silence is deafening, that's OK, too—that can be funny. Try the joke later with a different group. Your confidence will grow, and the laughs will come.

**Q. Can expressive body language help me generate laughter?**

**A.** Yes! I have worked with over a hundred professional comedians. They don't just tell a joke; they sell it. This means investing yourself—voice, heart, hand gestures—in your humor. Your conviction is what matters most. If you believe a joke's funny, chances are your audience will, too. Reminder: Don't laugh at your own jokes. Let *them* react first.

**Q. What are some ways to leverage a story to get my ideas across?**

**A.** Two approaches are helpful here. First, know the point you want to make before crafting your story. Second, make your tale a humorous *illustration* of your message.

**Q. How can humor help me manage upsets and conflicts?**

**A.** It's nearly impossible to feel angry while laughing. Try it sometime. If Lincoln could tell a funny story during the Civil War, you can take a moment to relax and recharge your team with a joke or funny quotation, even when the printer goes down. The key is to create time and space for humor. When I got angry as a kid, my mom invited me to count to ten, which helped me calm down. As a leader, you can't ask your team to count to ten, but you can use positive humor to create a calming breather for them.

> *Shared laughter creates a strong sense of togetherness.*

**Q. Should I use humor to address tough topics in my work?**

**A.** Shakespeare nailed it with this line in *King Lear*: "Jesters do oft prove prophets." Humor is a great way to communicate hard truths. For managers, mixing wit and warmth can be a tremendous tool for handling tough situations. Dynamic leaders use humor to address hard topics and make everyone feel more comfortable. However, be cautious. As I've discussed in this book, humor should unite, not offend. If you're unsure whether a joke might be offensive, remember my rule: If in doubt, leave it out.

**Q. How can I use humor to boost my confidence in social situations?**

**A.** The key is simple. First, smile. You will instantly look and feel good! Enjoying others' humor and laughing along makes you more approachable and builds connections. This type of friendly and fun engagement eases social interactions and boosts your confidence. When the time feels right, naturally add your own humor. It reinforces your sense of belonging. Share a favorite joke or witty remark linked to the conversation with a casual, "Hey, that reminds me of a story . . ."

**Q. How can I use laughter to create a sense of camaraderie with my group?**

**A.** That's easy—get them laughing *together*. Whether it's through a karaoke night, a dad joke competition, a costume party, or by hiring a clean comedian for an event, shared laughter creates a strong sense of togetherness. Pack them in close to each other in a room, then watch the feeling of unity and friendship grow as they enjoy the experience together.

**Q. What's the best way to use a joke or funny story to open or close my speech?**

**A.** The ways you start and end a talk are crucial. Make sure the joke or story is genuinely funny. Test it on friends and family *before* going public. Your funny piece must fit the purpose of your speech. An opening joke should set the tone for your talk and advance your message. Your closing story should be a humorous reminder of the core of your message. Oh, and one more thing: It should strike a chord in your listeners' hearts.

**Q. Can I use humor to draw people out and encourage them to talk?**

**A.** The best way to get someone to talk is to listen to them. The quickest way to listen is to *ask a question* and attentively tune in to the person's response. A touch of humor can make this enjoyable. For example, you might say, "I have two questions for you. What's your take on this proposal? And why is 'abbreviation' such a looooong word? Feel free to answer in either order." This blend of lightheartedness and genuine interest can help make your people more comfortable and open to sharing in the conversation.

**Q. Can you point me to resources you recommend for adding humor to presentations?**

**A.** Yes! Follow Eva Rose Daniel on LinkedIn for speaking and humor tips. Visit Mike Lukas's blog at FunnyMuscle.com. Hire a funny pro like Scott Meltzer to help you punch up your next speech (email scottm@comedyindustries.com). If wordplay is your thing, you will love visiting DrMardy.com. And check out more of my free resources at the back of this book, available at TheLaughterFactor.com

**Q. How can I handle nervousness when I'm speaking?**

As my friend Doug Wicks told me about feeling nervous, "Good. That means you care."

That said, nervousness can be unsettling when you want to be at your best. So here are eight ways to overcome these jitters:

1. Focus on *them*. It's not about you—it's about what *they* need.
2. Turn nerves into fuel. Get those butterflies to fly in formation!
3. Connect before content. Build a bond with your group before diving in.

4. Take deep breaths. Calm yourself with steady, deep breathing.
5. Skip the dry mouth drama. Pop a soothing lozenge before you speak (I use ACT Dry Mouth Lozenges).
6. Flash a smile. It makes them—and you—feel good.
7. Kick off strong! Nail your opening, and the rest will flow naturally.
8. Spot a friendly face.

Let me say a few more things about that last tip . . .

When you're speaking to a larger group, how can you still connect? Here's what it's like for me. I'm on the platform in a room full of three hundred people, and I observe the following:

▼ Sixty-seven people are scrolling their phones.
▼ Fourteen are coughing like they're auditioning for a NyQuil commercial.
▼ One guy is laughing way too loud (*looking at you, Carl*).

But then there's *one person—the face I focus on.*

A heartfelt shout-out, a nod to the coffee-clutcher, or a quick smile at someone attentive in the front row—it's all about recognizing *one individual.* That moment of connection and laughter ripples outward.

Focus on one person, then watch how the whole group lights up.

## The Last Laugh

What happens when you experience the laughter factor? It's like that whimsical floating-up-to-the-ceiling scene with Uncle Albert in *Mary Poppins*—laughter lifts us.

One of my humor heroes is Ed Wynn, the actor who played Uncle Albert. He had these words printed on his gravestone:

DEAR GOD:
THANKS.

*—Ed Wynn*

Imagine that winsome scene, but sung today with lyrics that super-charge your group's well-being.

We love to laugh

It's good for you and me

We yearn to laugh

It makes you feel healthy

And when we laugh

It builds up community.

Are you raising the spirits of your people? With the right tone of humor and fun, your team will feel like they can fly.

## Humor Being

As a human being, remember you are also a "humor" being.

I discovered a smile at the center of the universe.

*—Pierre Teilhard de Chardin*

Now let's recap. Let me tell ya what I told ya:

**Surprise!** Catch people off guard with something nobody sees coming—spring into action with the unexpected.

**Poke.** Start by making fun of yourself, then lightly roast those around you.

**In-Jokes.** Spread the glue that makes us want to stick together. Encourage shared humor that invites everybody in.

**Wordplay.** Dazzle us with clever twists of the tongue—share witty sayings and terribly funny puns. And don't forget the dad jokes.

**Amplify.** Go *big* and get big laughs. Turn problems into punch lines. Exaggerate your stories and jokes. Heighten the humor!

Why are these humor tactics so powerful? Why should you focus on the laughter factor?

Because humor isn't just a side dish—it's the secret sauce that leaves everyone wanting more. And the best part? It's on the house. These five tactics aren't just about getting laughs—they're about making life more enjoyable for you and the people you lead. And don't forget: The fun is for you, too.

## When You Laugh, You Last

Ashleigh Brilliant—yes, that's a real person—is living proof that humor keeps you going. At ninety-one years old, Mr. Brilliant is still using his wonderful sense of humor to inspire and entertain. Here are a few of Ashleigh's "brilliant" thoughts:

Everybody is entitled to my opinion.

My mind is open, by appointment only.

I feel much better, now that I've given up hope.

My hope for you? That humor becomes your lens on life. Live laughing, die laughing, and hey—why not laugh after death, too?

Laughter thrives when we're together. Whatever your humor style, share it. Lord Byron, the rebellious and sometimes funny poet, once said:

All who joy would win must share it.
Happiness was born a twin.

And let me remind you: It's the ability to *take* a joke, not just *make* one, that makes you a wonderful *humor being*.

## The Big Secret

You already have a sense of humor. Now, let *us* experience it. Remember, everyone around you—family, friends, customers, teammates, students, community members—is forever striving to think well of themselves. So are you. So am I.

Sending and receiving laughs makes us all feel better about who we are.

In the end, the laughter fades. It always does. After you crack 'em up, you'll probably find yourself back at your computer, staring at the screen. It's normal to feel a bit of a drop-off after the high of humor. Just an hour ago, you were connecting, lifting spirits, and spreading joy.

But here's the thing: the party isn't over! Laughter is the gift that keeps on giving—when you share it again and again. With the five humor tactics we have discovered together, you've got the tools to do just that.

Thanks for joining me on this journey. Humor is a bridge, and we've met across these pages. I hope to see you again on the bright side of the road.

One last thing—and it's the biggest secret in this entire book.

*You* are the laughter factor.

# ACKNOWLEDGMENTS

Thanks first of all to my trailblazing wife, Barb. I love you.

With big love and thanks to our amazing children, Leanna, Randy, Katie, and James—and their wonderful spouses and partners: Steamer, Janiece, and Tak.

And cheers to our joy-making grandsons, Micah and Brycen.

Special love and thanks to my mom and dad, Paul and Marianne, who showed me how to cherish a loving (and funny!) family.

To my sisters and brothers-in-law, Diana and Louis, Shelly and Mark, Mike and Kim, and my wonderful parents-in-law, John and Dorothy.

I'm lucky to have a right hand in Masha "Blaze" Rose, who contributed so much to *The Laughter Factor*, including the design of the five humor tactic icons. She brings "rocket fuel" to my work.

Thanks to Ally Carlton for helping me craft the proposal and early draft of this book. I appreciate Jennifer "Jen the Pen" Wallace for her contributions, and Kristi Hein, my "secret weapon" editor.

With love to all my dear colleagues and friends at Westfall Gold— they are a second family to me. And much appreciation to Parable Talent, Big Speak, and LeaderPass. I love partnering with you to surprise and delight people across North America and beyond.

I'm grateful to mentors and coaches, including Diana Zimmerman, Barbara Daoust, Jay Mincks, Erol Fox, Jen Laffin, and Becky Robinson.

Thanks to friends: Michael Levine; David O'Shaughnessy; Doug Wicks; David Donovan; Chris Dorman; Bruce and Angela Scott; Mike, Diana, and Jessica Irvin; April Floria; Lisa Wolf; Tiffany Heck; Bob and Kim Westfall; Sarah Richards; "Snag" Naglich; "Pearlia" Flannery; Allison Rickard; Anna Birkby; Carissa Craven; Richard Narramore; Jeff Civillico; Ron Forseth; Mark Matlock; Wayne Clark; Tom Sweeny; Tamika Hunter; Travis Coyne; Scott Derrickson; Nick Arnette; Greg Bennick; Bob Korljan; Dave and Beth Stone; Chris Blackmore; Pete McLeod; Charles Berry; Danny Adams; Amy Eddy; Christa Haberstock; Lisa Carnemolla Comerford; and Lena Otto.

I want to express special gratitude to Aaron and Hailey O'Brien, Sheryl Moon, Randy Bateman, Cliff Sarcona, Brian McElreath, Cameron Carrillo, Liam O'Shea, Cary Trivanovich, David Doyle, David Laflin, Eva Rose Daniel, Kathy Westfield, Ken Felig, Luke Tai, Mark Joseph, Mark Matsumoto, Nazareth Rizkallah, Nick and Susan Lewin, Ross Kimball, Ruben Padilla, Scott and Yoney Wood, Steve Barnes, Tim Filmore, Alistair and Susan Begg, Mark and Lucy Green, Burt and Carolyn Rosen, Nde Nkimbeng, Les Mazon, Duane Cashin, Michael Joiner, and Bill Jones.

A big shoutout to the "Creek Parkers"—Brian aka "Rail" and Tammye, Clowie, Cotty, Noj, Grego, and Samantha—for years of fun and friendship.

Heartfelt thanks to Dan Balow, my literary agent; my media team at Smith Publicity; Estelle Lloyd with Westchester Publishing Services; and a huge thanks to Neal Maillet; Jeevan Sivasubramaniam (the kindest curmudgeon I know); Ashley Ingram, who designed the book cover; Katelyn Keating; Christy Kirk; Kristen Frantz; Elsa Frantz; and the entire community of publishing pros and leadership authors at Berrett-Koehler Publishers. Your guidance brought *The Laughter Factor* to life.

I am grateful to my "Humor Heroes": Ann Tatarelli Ulrich, Mary Anne Kristan, Karith Foster, Dr. Mardy Grothe, Mike Lukas, Scott Meltzer, and Katrine Spang-Hanssen.

I appreciate John Maxwell, Tom De Vries, and Leanne Ely for their endorsements, and my pal Bob Goff for cheering me on.

This book is dedicated to the memory of my dad, Paul D. Brown, who passed before it was released. He showed me how to tell great jokes. But more than that, he showed up for all of us. I couldn't have asked for a better father.

Finally, thank you, dear reader, for laughing and learning with me.

# INDEX

# WORK WITH ADAM

### Bring your people together!

Hire Adam Christing to speak at your next annual gathering, business confer-ence, or kickoff program. His engaging keynotes are audience favorites:

### Leading with Laughter

Experience how positive humor ele-vates leadership, energizes teams, and fosters a culture of *HAuthenticity*.

### Discover Your Laugh Language

Everyone has a laugh language—a unique way of connecting through humor. Harness your smile strategies and turn communication into connection.

### You Can Do Magic!

Your team will love this *experiential* keynote, combining interactive magic and practical motivation. Celebrate the fun of teamwork and personal empowerment.

"It's not easy to find a funny keynote speaker who can share a super message and delight our team with laughter."

—*Julie Castongia, Senior Director, Optum*

## Make your event an extraordinary experience!

Schedule Adam as the Master of Ceremonies for your meeting, awards show, gala, or special event.

"Adam Christing is the Tom Brady of emcees!"

—*Mark Green, International Executive, EXXON*

Connect with Adam:
AdamChristing.com

## Visit TheLaughterFactor.com for free humor resources and some surprises!

▼ Sign up for Adam's "Laugh for a Change" weekly newsletter.
▼ Connect with Adam Christing on LinkedIn.
▼ Follow @AdamChristing on social media.
▼ Book Adam for your next gathering. Send an email to: Hello@AdamChristing.com.

Discover More:
TheLaughterFactor.com

# ABOUT THE AUTHOR

Adam Christing got hooked on the power of laughter at fourteen when he was hired to perform a comedy-magic show at a birthday party. That moment sparked a lifelong passion for humor—not just as entertainment but as a superpower that links, lifts, and leads people.

Today, Adam is a sought-after keynote speaker, award-winning event emcee, and interactive comedian who has created community through laughter for more than a million people across forty-nine states and internationally in Canada, Mexico, Europe, and China. As president of *Clean Comedians*, he has spent three decades helping organizations bring people together with positive humor.

He earned a degree in public speaking from Biola University, where he was named into the university's "Alumni Hall of Fame." His work has been featured in *The New York Times*, *The Wall Street Journal*, and *Success* magazine. He's shared the stage with business icons, bestselling authors, a former US president, and celebrities like Alice Cooper, Martin Short, and *America's Got Talent* host Terry Crews. Adam has appeared on more than 100 podcasts and TV programs, including *Entertainment Tonight*, CNN, and Fox News.

Adam lives in beautiful Western North Carolina with his wife, Barb. They have four kids and two grandsons who keep them laughing.

# Berrett–Koehler
## Publishers

**Berrett-Koehler** is an independent publisher dedicated to an ambitious mission: *Connecting people and ideas to create a world that works for all.*

Our publications span many formats, including print, digital, audio, and video. We also offer online resources, training, and gatherings. And we will continue expanding our products and services to advance our mission.

We believe that the solutions to the world's problems will come from all of us, working at all levels: in our society, in our organizations, and in our own lives. Our publications and resources offer pathways to creating a more just, equitable, and sustainable society. They help people make their organizations more humane, democratic, diverse, and effective (and we don't think there's any contradiction there). And they guide people in creating positive change in their own lives and aligning their personal practices with their aspirations for a better world.

And we strive to practice what we preach through what we call "The BK Way." At the core of this approach is *stewardship,* a deep sense of responsibility to administer the company for the benefit of all of our stakeholder groups, including authors, customers, employees, investors, service providers, sales partners, and the communities and environment around us. Everything we do is built around stewardship and our other core values of *quality, partnership, inclusion,* and *sustainability.*

We are grateful to our readers, authors, and other friends who are supporting our mission. We ask you to share with us examples of how BK publications and resources are making a difference in your lives, organizations, and communities at bkconnection.com/impact.

Dear reader,

Thank you for picking up this book and welcome to the worldwide BK community! You're joining a special group of people who have come together to create positive change in their lives, organizations, and communities.

## What's BK all about?

Our mission is to connect people and ideas to create a world that works for all.

Why? Our communities, organizations, and lives get bogged down by old paradigms of self-interest, exclusion, hierarchy, and privilege. But we believe that can change. That's why we seek the leading experts on these challenges—and share their actionable ideas with you.

## A welcome gift

To help you get started, we'd like to offer you a **free copy** of one of our bestselling ebooks:

**bkconnection.com/welcome**

When you claim your **free ebook**, you'll also be subscribed to our blog.

## Our freshest insights

Access the best new tools and ideas for leaders at all levels on our blog at ideas.bkconnection.com.

Sincerely,

Your friends at Berrett-Koehler